9

D1711245

ᗡ947.

LIFE IN RUSSIA
UNDER CATHERINE THE GREAT

(overleaf) *The bridge of boats over the Neva, St Petersburg*

LIFE IN RUSSIA
UNDER CATHERINE
THE GREAT

Miriam Kochan

European Life Series
Edited by Peter Quennell

London: B. T. BATSFORD LTD
New York: G. P. PUTNAM'S SONS

Acknowledgment

The author and publishers would like to thank the following for the illustrations appearing in this book: the Trustees of the British Museum for pages 48–9, 52–3, 72 and 148; Harvard University Press, publishers of *Journey from St Petersburg to Moscow* by A. N. Radishchev, 1958, for page 146; Hermitage State Museum, Leningrad for page 44; the Honourable Baron Dimsdale for page 12; Professor D. Lang for pages 143 and 144; Librairie Ernest Leroux, publishers of *La Vie et les Mœurs en Russie de Pierre le Grand à Lenine* by G. K. Loukomski, 1928 for pages 28–9, 78–9 and 112–13; Mansell Collection for pages 10, 12, 16–17, 42–3, 45, 47, 51, 54–5, 57, 152–3 and 156–7; Mrs Evelyn Marindin for page 11; Mrs Herbert May Collection, Washington for page 131; Radio Times Hulton Picture Library for pages 2, 3, 4, 5, 7, 13, 15, 25, 33, 34–5, 37, 38, 62, 83, 91, 98, 107, 108–9, 111, 132, 133, 138, 140, 142, 150, 160 and 171.

The author and publishers would also like to thank Macmillan & Co. Ltd for permission to quote from their book, *The Russian Journals of Martha and Catherine Wilmot*, 1803–8, published in 1934.

Made and printed in Great Britain
by Jarrold & Sons Ltd, Norwich
for the publishers
B. T. BATSFORD LTD
4 Fitzhardinge Street London W1
G. P. PUTNAM'S SONS
200 Madison Avenue New York NY 10016

Contents

The Illustrations

The Illustrations

The Illustrations

The Illustrations

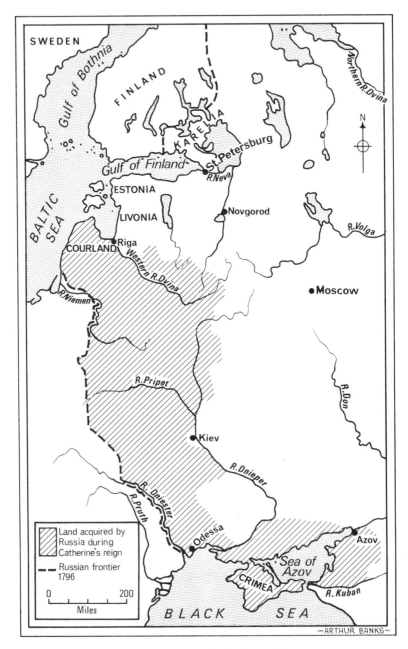

The Russian Empire in 1796

Introduction: a European Power

At the end of the seventeenth century, Russia in European eyes was a vast Asiatic desert, inhabited by long-robed, long-bearded savages, ruled from the eastern domes and cupolas of the Moscow Kremlin. At the beginning of the nineteenth century, Russia was a leading European power of major importance in the struggle to restore peace to the West.

How had this transformation taken place? How, within the space of a century, had a barbarous country been accepted as a western realm? The eighteenth century marked a momentous and dramatic phase in Russian development. The reign of Catherine the Great, which occupied the years from 1762 to 1796, witnessed a vital stage in this startling change.

It is difficult to ascertain whether the Russian attempt to transform itself into a western power was the cause or the result of its acceptance by the European nations in the eighteenth century. Russia's importance was generally acknowledged during the rule of Peter the Great and consolidated and extended under Catherine.

This recognition resulted in part from the increasing importance of Russia as a military power to be reckoned with. At the end of the seventeenth century, the Russian army was neither efficient, professional, nor particularly large. By the last years of Peter the Great, it was one of the most powerful in Europe. Its victory at Poltava in 1709 over the Swedes, a credit to the Russian Empire, had already brought to the country the prestige that only a military victory could give. In 1757, this army gave conclusive proof of its ability, and in so doing astounded the western world, by defeating the Prussian army, renowned for its military efficiency, at Gross Jägerndorf. The Empress Catherine continued the policy of expanding the army: in 1731 it numbered 132,000 men; by 1796, it had risen to 458,000.

Not only did Russia become a military power, her navy was also expanded to become an efficient weapon of war. By the time of Peter's death in 1725 Russia had developed into one of the great naval powers of

I

Peter the Great defeating Sweden at the battle of Poltava in 1709

Europe. Here again, Catherine continued his policy. When the Russian fleet appeared in the Mediterranean and inflicted a shattering defeat on the Turks at Chesme, off Chios, in the 1760s, all Europe realised that Russia was to be feared at sea as well as on land.

Russia's importance in the eighteenth century could not, however, be measured by brute force alone. In 1695, when Peter the Great first acquired effective control of government, Russia had no permanent diplomatic representatives in foreign capitals. By 1721, she had 21 permanent diplomatic missions in foreign countries; by 1779, it had fallen, but only slightly, to 19. Simultaneously, the number of foreign diplomats more or less permanently resident in Russia increased: in 1702, there were four; by 1719 eleven.

All these factors meant that Russia was capable of carrying out a more vigorous and more continuous foreign policy and of doing so through the media the western world understood. The foreign policy followed was one of territorial expansion. The Mongol invasions of the thirteenth century had reduced Russia to a very small area of Muscovite land surrounding Moscow. From the fifteenth century to the eighteenth, Russian policy had represented an extension of this land—to north, south and east, where conquests could be made at the expense of nomadic peoples. Her frontier to the west from the Baltic almost to the Black Sea was occupied by organised states. Those with a Baltic coastline were Livonia and Estonia and beyond them, the Duchy of Courland with its long Baltic shore. Further on, lay Poland, and then the Balkan peninsula, the territory of the Turks in Europe.

Peter the Great, with an eye always on the West, began seriously to turn his attention to these western frontiers. When he joined Denmark and Saxony in their attack on the Swedish Empire in 1700 he brought Russia into closer political contact with western Europe than ever before. His victory at Poltava made Russian influence dominant in Poland and opened up prospects of control of much of the Baltic coastline and even parts of northern Germany. In 1721, the Treaty of Nystadt ended the long struggle against Sweden and gave Russia Estonia and Livonia (with the ports of Revel and Riga and their access to the Baltic) as well as Karelia, and established her as a Baltic power.

An insignificant factor at the end of the seventeenth century,

Russian victory over the Turkish fleet at Tschere in 1770

Peter the Great

Potemkin

Catherine receiving the Ottoman envoys

Russia at the death of Peter the Great was feared by her neighbours and counted as a military and political equal by the great powers in Europe, even if she was not recognised in cultural or economic terms.

Catherine continued Peter's policy of expansion westwards. In 1768 Turkish rule was still supreme all round the Black Sea and its peninsula. The Turks controlled the northern shore, and also therefore the lower reaches and mouths of the Dnieper, the Bug and the Dniester—and to control the mouths of the rivers was to control river trade. By the end of Catherine's reign, though she did not (as she and her lover Potemkin had once dreamed) rule over Constantinople, she had acquired the Crimea,

Stanislaus Poniatowski

the Kuban and Terek areas, the Black Sea steppe between the Bug and the Dnieper and freedom of navigation in the Black Sea.

Finally, Poland had always been regarded as a hindrance if not a danger to the growth of the Russian state. Catherine at first envisaged a united Poland subject to the guidance and influence of Russia. With this end in view, in 1764 she placed a discarded lover, Stanislaus Poniatowski, on the Polish throne, with the backing of Russian gold and troops. As events proceeded, however, Poland became a pawn in the fight for power in Turkey, and from 1772 onwards repeated divisions of the country resulted in Russian territorial gains: at the first partition in 1772, she gained land east of the Rivers Dwina and Dnieper; at the second in 1793, Russia took an extensive slice of territory in Lithuania and White Russia, including part of the Polish area of the Ukraine; at the third in 1795, she added the Duchy of Courland, the rest of Lithuania and Vilna to her domains.

Russia's emergence as a European power was confirmed by marked improvements in her diplomatic status. In 1779, the war between Austria and Prussia over the Bavarian succession was ended by Russo-French

5

mediation. Russia was a guarantor of the settlement and therefore for the first time achieved a formal *locus standi* in German affairs. However, already the year before, the French representative to the Imperial Diet had complained that Russia—and not, as had been the case for the last one and a half centuries, France—was now the dominant foreign influence in the politics of Germany.

Russia's growing importance was also apparent in 1780 when the Armed Neutrality was formed under Russian leadership. The Neutrality had little practical effect, but nonetheless helped to consolidate in western Europe the impression of Russian power, which had been developing since Poltava and Gross Jägerndorf. Her brilliant military victories and territorial acquisitions had gained her the position of the arbiter of Europe, respected and feared by Prussia and Austria on land, and by Britain and France at sea.

The partition of Poland

Similarly, by extending her territories, Russia experienced a period of economic expansion which made her of consequence to the West. Population increased as much from the addition of new provinces as from natural causes. Under the stimulus, agriculture and industry did likewise. What Russia lacked as a result of her slow adoption of improved methods of farming and manufacture was amply made good by her great quantitative wealth. The exports she could offer to the West, particularly of iron, made her an interesting factor in world commerce.

Concomitant with this entry of Russia into the West was an attempt by her rulers to transform the face of the nation from

Asiatic mongol to civilised western. Peter the Great was the first Russian monarch to set foot outside his frontiers for many a long century. He returned to his capital armed not only with increased knowledge of western techniques, but also with many western technicians. On his direction, Russian youths were sent to the West to acquire new skills. This practice was not always entirely satisfactory. Admiral Sir Cyprian Bridge comments: 'Upon their recall, undergoing a strict examination, they were found, instead of attaining the rudiments of a seaman, to have acquired only the insignificant accomplishments of fine gentlemen.' Peter did not,

Peter the Great cutting the beard of a boyar

however, regard these accomplishments as so insignificant. He showed his firm determination that his country should not only be a western power, it should also look like one.

In pursuit of this purpose, among other measures he ordered his nobles to cut off their beards—and if they refused, cut them off himself—and wear western dress. Along the same lines he had published in 1717 a translarion of a German pamphlet, *The Honourable Mirror of Youth*. This set out detailed rules for the conduct of a Russian gentleman: youths must doff their hats to acquaintances at three paces' distance; they must not pick their noses or clean their teeth with a knife; they should spit to one side and not in the midst of a group; they must not wolf their food, put their elbows on the table or scratch their heads; they must not wear heavy boots when dancing; nor must young ladies speak Russian in the presence of servants. He also built the Empire a brand-new western capital, St Petersburg, on a site at the swampy

Peterhof

mouth of the Neva, and here he transferred his court from the old 'Asiatic' capital of Moscow. Side by side with the rejection of old Muscovy, went his subjection of the Orthodox Church. Ruled by its Patriarch, it was extremely conservative and hostile to foreign influences, and presented a major obstacle to the westernisation of the country. Peter abolished the office of Patriarch and replaced it by a college similar in kind to those used for secular administration. He laid the foundations for the subjection of church to state. Catherine continued the process. As we shall see later, she closed down the monasteries on a massive scale and instead made the cities the main centres of Russian culture.

Peter's courtiers were already feeling themselves to be culturally superior Europeans, able to deride those lacking the advantages of western refinement. In this vein, the poet Istornin wrote:

America is wilfully rapacious,
Her people savage in morals and rule . . .
Knowing no God, evil in thought
No one can accomplish anything
Where such stupidity, vileness and sin prevail.

This trend continued under Catherine. Not content with limiting westernisation to physical externals, she aimed also at creating an intellectual image of Russian enlightenment. She may have realised that the western attitude to Russia was formed not only by the behaviour of Russian citizens abroad, nor yet entirely by the appearance of capital, court and nobility at home. It was also influenced by the mode of government it employed. It was felt in Europe that the moral and intellectual defects of the Russians were at least partially produced by the regime under which they lived. Macartney wrote: 'The form of government is, and will always be, the principal cause of the want of virtue and genius in this country, as making the motives of one and the rewards of both, depend upon accident and caprice.' The despotism of the Russian monarch was furthermore, in western eyes, an indication that Russia was an Oriental and not a European power. The Empress was not prepared to sacrifice her role of despot to the cause of westernisation. But she corresponded at length and in depth with western philosophes and published laws and treatises calculated to impress Europe with the picture of an enlightened monarch reigning, kindly and wisely, in accordance with western-style principles.

Not that physical externals were neglected during her reign. The process of westernisation, in reaching an unprecedented peak, not only embraced the world of thought, but also all aspects of daily life. Besides becoming the official language of her court, French was also the medium for polite social intercourse. Western dress was general amongst the noble classes; western education was *de rigueur*; and St Petersburg, the new capital, was filled with western buildings of unbounded magnificence—a wondrous monument to impress the western traveller.

St Petersburg, showing the statue of Peter the Great and the Senate

But in numbering Russia among the European powers in the second half of the eighteenth century, we must not be misled. Although the court of St Petersburg could compare with any court in contemporary Europe and though the Russian diplomat could meet his colleagues as an equal abroad, Russia internally still differed greatly from the rest of Europe. In the first place, a change of this magnitude could not take place overnight, or even within the space of a hundred years. In the same way as the hastily built capital of St Petersburg had been constructed from nothing on the Neva

Martha Wilmot, friend of Princess Dashkov

marshes, so this European façade covered the Asiatic face of the nation. It could not be more than a façade. Much more time was needed before the change could remotely affect the great body of the Russian people. It transformed the court, it affected the nobility, it left the mass of the common people untouched. Even with the court and nobility, it could only alter the externals of their lives. They spoke French, they ate French dishes, they wore French fashions and, in so doing, they considered that they were Europeans. But they thought like Asiatics and time and time again the memoirs of the period mention the uncouthness of their behaviour and how uneasily they wore their western finery.

If westernisation could only be superficial with them, it was even less likely that it could have any effect on the lower levels of society. The greater proportion of the nation still lived tied in a state of bondage to

Catherine II   *Princess Dashkov*

the nobles, in conditions not experienced in most European countries since the Middle Ages. The efforts of the monarchs had made possible a jump of many centuries in the superficial standards of the upper classes, so that they seemed at least to be living comparable lives to those of their European contemporaries. The condition of the serfs had remained more or less static and had, if anything, registered some degree of deterioration as a result of the westernisation of the upper ranks. Redoubled efforts were required from servile labour to maintain the free few in their western elegance at St Petersburg. The difference between the two basic classes of society was so greatly increased that contact between the European, eighteenth-century master and his Asiatic, medieval serf was reduced almost to nothing.

Simultaneously with the great interest that Russia was taking in the West, there arose a similar, though by no means corresponding, interest by the West in Russia. This is not to say that Russian culture or *mores* had any appreciable influence on western thought at that time. But Russia was now on the map. It came to be included in the grand tours undertaken by the sprigs of the nobility for educational purposes. The

Elizabeth I   *Peter III, Catherine's husband*

glory and glamour of St Petersburg spread widely by repute and attracted sightseers to the court. Many contemporary accounts, travel-ogues and letters were published by these 'tourists' on their return to Britain and this in itself bears witness to the prevalent interest. William Richardson, for example, accompanied Lord Cathcart to St Petersburg in the dual capacity of tutor and secretary. He remained there from 1768 to 1772 before returning to occupy the Chair of Humanity at Glasgow University for the rest of his life. His *Anecdotes of the Russian Empire*, published in London in 1784, are an invaluable source of information on the way of life in the country during this period of change.

Similarly, two young, well-educated Irish girls, the Misses Catherine and Martha Wilmot, spent several years in Russia living with the Princess Dashkov, one of the closest friends of the Empress Catherine in her youth. A collection of extracts from their letters and diaries during this period has been published relatively recently and makes fascinating reading. Archdeacon William Coxe in his youth went as travelling tutor to a young nobleman, George Lord Herbert, on the grand tour and later produced his *Travels into Poland, Russia, Sweden and Denmark*. Finally,

13

Introduction: a European Power

Robert Ker Porter went to Russia in 1803 as historical painter to the Emperor, Alexander I of Russia. Though his visit occurred a few years after Catherine's death, many of his comments remain valid for the period under review.

At the same time, there was a significant awakening of Russian interest in Russia itself, sponsored and encouraged by the Empress. She sent out many expeditions to survey her country and its frontiers and so acquire social, geographical and agricultural information. Her mania for collecting data on her own country was also shown in the orders and instructions she sent out to her provincial governors, and in her repeated censuses of the population. (All this effort, it must be noted, has not furnished adequate statistics which can be quoted with confidence by the modern historian, and figures included in this book do no more than indicate the general trend.)

Before proceeding to a detailed study of the way of life in Russia during the reign of Catherine the Great, it is relevant to take a closer look at the monarch herself and the circumstances surrounding her accession to the throne of Russia. For Catherine herself was not, by birth, Russian; nor had she any legal claim to the Russian throne. She was born Sophie Augusta Frederika, the daughter of a petty German prince, Christian August of Anhalt-Zerbst, the Governor of Stettin, and of Princess Johanna Elizabeth of Holstein-Gottorp. Her upbringing befitted her for the role of minor importance that seemed inevitably to be hers.

To find how so great a change in her circumstances occurred, we must turn to Russia, where Elizabeth, daughter of Peter the Great, was ruling in solitary splendour. Elizabeth had never married—which is not to say that she did not have at least one known lover—and therefore had no direct heir to name as her successor. To fill the gap, she selected her nephew Karl Peter Ulrich, the orphaned Duke of Schleswig-Holstein-Gottorp. Peter was heir presumptive to the throne of Sweden and was being brought up to this end in the Lutheran faith and educated in Swedish and Latin. Now he was wrenched from his familiar surroundings, taken to St Petersburg and forcibly instructed in Russian ways and customs. Elizabeth chose as a wife for him the young Sophie Augusta Frederika. Sophie, in her turn, was brought to Russia, baptised afresh as Catherine Alexandrovna, received into the Orthodox Church (her own upbringing had been strictly Lutheran) and married to Peter (also newly baptised Grand Duke Peter Feodorovitch).

But the marriage was doomed from the start. Peter, if not an entirely stupid young man (and opinions vary on the extent of his stupidity), was quite unfitted for the great task which lay ahead of him. He is said to have much preferred playing with toy soldiers to adult occupations. Things military were always his paramount interest: his passion for German uniforms, rather than the traditional Russian ones, was closely linked to his slavish admiration for Frederick of Prussia. The

Gregory Orlov, who helped Catherine to power

young couple proved incompatible from the start, and their union was made no happier by the many restrictions Elizabeth placed on the 'young court'. They were kept isolated from all affairs of any importance to the state and a watch was kept on every detail of their private lives. Catherine, thrown back upon her own considerable resources, spent her time most profitably, learning to be more Russian than the Russians (she devoted much energy to learning the Russian language), wooing the favour of the people around her and reading widely (particularly amongst the authors of the French Enlightenment such as Montesquieu). Now it was that the great strength of her character became apparent—her forcefulness, her quiet determination to rule, her charm which could win her friends in the most unlikely circles.

On the death of Elizabeth in 1762, Peter duly ascended the throne of

(overleaf) *Coronation of Catherine the Great*

Introduction: a European Power

Russia. He seems almost to have courted the unpopularity of his subjects, while Catherine had been building up a store of supporters. The measures he passed immediately after his coronation unfailingly aroused displeasure in one or other of the areas of power: he abruptly ended the war with Germany at a time when it seemed that Russia must triumph; he acted consistently against the church—he forbade the maintenance of private chapels, ordered the clergy to remove all icons from the churches, ordained that ecclesiastics must wear secular dress and deprived the church of its lands; he behaved in an unseemly fashion at religious ceremonies—even at his own coronation he was said to have thumbed his nose, if not put out his tongue, at the archbishop; his treatment of his wife could not meet with general approval; and finally, it was generally known (for he had never attempted to conceal the fact) that he

Catherine acknowledging the crowds from the balcony of the unfinished **Winter Palace**

felt no interest in Russia but considered himself a Holsteiner through and through.

The rift between the couple had grown so great—Catherine had her lovers, Peter his acknowledged mistress—that there was even talk of divorce. In any case he was openly abusive to his wife in public. But Catherine, or rather her devoted followers, the four Orlov brothers, acted first. In the same year that Peter had ascended the throne Catherine triumphantly deposed her husband and rode to St Petersburg, accompanied by her noble guard regiments, to be crowned

Medal struck on Catherine's accession

Catherine II amidst the loud acclaim of her subjects. The unlucky Peter was imprisoned and shortly afterwards murdered in a scuffle, probably by an Orlov brother, possibly with Catherine's connivance. Thereafter, there was always the feeling that she had to redeem herself in the eyes of Europe for this crime.

Thus, four facts of paramount importance must be borne in mind throughout our study of Russia in the second half of the eighteenth century: the persistence of the institution of serfdom whereby the majority of the inhabitants were the property of a small minority; the recent emergence of the country from a state of Asiatic and medieval somnolence to that of a major European power; the uncertainty of the Empress Catherine's position on the throne—she was, apart from anything else, a foreigner in a strange land—which inevitably influenced her actions and forced her to curry favour of those best able to maintain her on it; and finally, the very size of the Russian Empire which, apart from anything else, makes it extremely difficult to treat it as a whole. The attempt to do so has meant to a very large extent ignoring local particularities between the peoples of each area and concentrating solely on major national trends.

1   Enlightened Despotism

Catherine herself exemplifies the strange results of the application of western ideas to the Russian state. Nourished on the theories of the western philosophers, she seems to have assumed the throne of this autocracy, little aware of the paradox of her situation.

The conflict was uneven. In the first place, the theory and structure of Russian government offered particular scope for the exercise of benevolent despotism. The position of the crown in Russia in relation to the nation at large assumed and provided for the wielding of absolute power by a ruler whom the people regarded as the head of an enormous family. To them, he was not only 'little father' in the full sense of the term, but also an emperor with autocratic powers. Government took the form of administration by a body of men responsible to the crown alone.

In the second place, autocracy came naturally to Catherine, and her convictions were strengthened by her interpretation of western philosophic ideas and ideals. This was the age of reason, the age of rulers instructed by philosophers who had no doubt that their will must be supreme. They worked with the happy conviction that this will was guided by the right principles, and that its exercise could not help but bring the maximum good to their people.

In the early days of her reign, before she had given up the unequal struggle between liberal ideas and autocratic facts, Catherine called together an assembly from the whole Empire to draw up a new code of law. She was motivated by the need to reduce the chaos of the machinery of government to some sort of order. It is significant to note in this context that all sectors of Russian society were represented on this commission, except the priesthood and the bonded serfs. Before the assembly gathered, Catherine spent two fruitful years preparing a set of Instructions, based on her years of reading of the philosophes. This *Nakaz* clearly reflects the influence of the ideas of Montesquieu's *Esprit des Lois* and Beccaria's *Crime and Punishment*.

The general line of thought is indicated by the opening pronouncement that 'Christian Law teaches people to do good one to another, as much as possibly can be done; that every honest man in the community will wish to see his country happy, glorious, safe and tranquil and himself to live under a law which protects, but does not oppress.' She elaborates this by explaining that any action which was considered prejudicial to either the community or the individual should be forbidden; that all should be equal in the sight of the law, that all must obey the law but also that all must be free to do all that the law does not forbid. So far, so good. The thinking shows an obvious acceptance of Locke's theory that law and freedom were necessary to one another, could not exist without each other—in other words, the concept of the freedom of the individual within an ordered society.

However, the Instructions contained two features which completely negated these high-flown principles. First, Catherine once again emphasised the absolutism of the crown—she stated that the sovereign was supreme, the sole source of all civil and political power, subject to no check. True, the sovereign was there to serve the people, but this service was solely dependent on his or her good intentions. Diderot wrote with full justification, 'the Empress of Russia is certainly a despot, since, whatever the true end of her government, it makes all liberty and property depend on one person.'

But the Instructions give a comprehensive defence of absolute monarchy.

'The Sovereign is absolute; for there is no other authority but that which centres in his single person, that can act with a vigour proportionate to the extent of such a vast dominion. . . . What is the true end of Monarchy? [the Empress asks]. Not to deprive people of their natural liberty; but to correct their actions in order to attain the supreme good. The intention and the end of monarchy is the glory of the citizen, of the State and of the Sovereign.'

The *Nakaz* was, in fact, a brave and early attempt to base imperial authority on philosophic principles rather than hereditary right or religious sanction. As Catherine had no hereditary right and precious little religious sanction, her aim is understandable.

Second, the Instructions committed themselves to the general term that serfdom should only exist in the interests of the state. Catherine urged the deputies to shun all occasions for further reduction of the people to slavery except in cases of dire necessity, but she opposed any general measure of emancipation. It should be a rare condition, but it would, however, be extremely dangerous to free all the serfs at once.

'We are obliged to alleviate the situation of the subjects as much as sound reason will permit. And therefore to shun all occasions of reducing people to a state of slavery, except the utmost necessity should inevitably oblige us to do it. However, it is still highly necessary to prevent those causes which so frequently incited slaves to rebel against their masters; but till these causes are discovered it is impossible to prevent the like accidents by laws; though the tranquillity both of the one and of the other depends upon it.'

Otherwise, the Instructions showed a fine humanitarian approach! The section on Crime and Punishment recommended that the prevention of crime should be conceded more importance than the infliction of punishment and that a distinction should be drawn between crimes of different natures and importance. Capital punishment should be reduced to the absolute minimum and torture completely prohibited. Elsewhere there are recommendations for more judicious methods of taxing the peasantry, for the encouragement of agriculture and for greater freedom of commerce with all peoples. The theme of religious toleration runs throughout the *Nakaz*.

The assembly sat for some 18 months. Many of the problems were intensively discussed. Many of the differences between its various representatives—the nobles and the merchants for example—were lengthily aired. But no new code of laws ever emerged and the assembly was dissolved having achieved nothing. This may perhaps be too superficial a dismissal. The detailed discussion of the assembly, although it resulted in no concrete benefit, did certainly put certain new and potentially subversive political ideas into circulation. The commission was broad enough in composition and representation to carry these ideas home with its members into every social group. The suggestion has even been made that they reached—albeit in a garbled form—the bonded peasantry and may have been indirectly responsible for the Pugachev revolt.

The Instructions aside, Catherine's policy in the early part of her reign showed many symptoms of enlightenment, although where her support of the nobility and her avoidance of the issue of serfdom were concerned, she remained consistently undemocratic. She engaged in no religious persecution and even offered refuge to the persecuted in other lands. In 1771, 26,000 refugees came to Russia. In 1785, her edict of toleration permitted freedom of worship to all creeds. She even gave official support to Mohammedanism.

In her immigration policy she made one notable exception to this rule: 'Immigrants of any nation, *the Jews excepted*' [author's italics] were invited to come and settle in Russia. For the rest, she pursued a consistent policy of encouraging immigration in the firm conviction that manpower was the foundation of national strength, offering gifts of land and settlement grants, together with the promise of several other privileges. An advertisement to this effect was translated into many foreign languages and printed in newspapers abroad. As far as Germans were concerned the advertisement proved fairly effective; many came. But Catherine's hope that the Russian peasants would learn agricultural economy from them was disappointed. They merely existed in isolation in lone pockets of disparate community life.

She was also much concerned with education. The success of her measures in this direction can be assessed from the fact that the numbers of children attending all types of schools in Russia rose from just over 4,000 in 1786 to nearly 18,000 in 1791. In 1764, she sent a commission to Britain to report on universities and schools and draw up instructions for the introduction into Russia of a new educational system. In 1782, a committee for the establishment of public schools was set up, and in 1786 she announced her intention of opening national schools for the education of children of all classes in every provincial and district capital town. Subjects taught were to include reading, writing, mathematics, history and geography, as well as natural history, physics and mechanics in the higher classes. However, these schools encountered certain difficulties. In the first place, they had to work on a very limited budget as their funds had to come from the provincial public welfare boards. Secondly, there was a shortage of children prepared to attend the schools and, even when the children would come, a shortage of teachers became apparent. A contemporary Academician, Henry Storch, related that

Enlightened Despotism

Petersburg in 1790 possessed 13 middle and inferior schools in which children of the 'common people' were taught, *inter alia*, reading, writing, arithmetic, Russian history and geography. But how 'common' the people were is a very moot point. In the same year, an upper school was also founded there.

Whatever the degree of success they enjoyed with the masses, Catherine's attempts succeeded in making education more general and of better quality for members of the merchant and noble classes. For example, a commercial college was opened for the sons of merchants which, when their course was completed, encouraged them to travel in Europe and imbibe first-hand knowledge of western trade conditions, always provided 'the parents consenting thereto'. Despite the fact that all expenses were met by the Treasury, very few parents did indeed accept this invitation. As far as the nobility was concerned, many of their schools owed their foundation to Catherine and all of them their expansion. They included, to name but two typical examples, the famous Land Cadet Corps College, which was established anew in 1766 as a military school, admitting 120 boys aged between five and six every three years. Prerequisites for entry were that the father must be a noble and the child enjoy perfect health. We shall have more to say of this establishment later. The Academy of Fine Arts admitted 325 sons of free parents annually, at the age of six, and during the following 12 years taught them painting, engraving, sculpture, music, architecture and the making of a variety of artificial and mechanical works, as well, of course, as reading, writing, arithmetic, French and German. Youths showing most talent and industry were sent to continue their studies abroad in England, Italy and France.

Catherine was also concerned with broadening the education of her own sex and one of her dearest undertakings was to convert the Voskresenskoi convent into a seminary for the education of young ladies. In all 480 girls were admitted annually at the age of six—half of noble, half of burgher descent—and the branches of knowledge in which they were brought up were adapted to accord with their future station in life. The syllabus included several languages (particularly French), the elements of religion, geography, history, epistolary writing, music, dancing, declamation and acting. The daughters of burghers were also brought up to do various kinds of work. It was hoped that when they left school, they would be of great value in diffusing a taste for a more refined way of life!

All branches of public service emerged from Catherine's reign

Men's hospital in 1740

improved. Every province of the Russian Empire was equipped with a tribunal under the name of the College of General Provision entrusted with the care of all establishments intended for the alleviation of human misery. To these belonged the public schools, orphan houses, hospitals and infirmaries, institutions for the poor, houses for incurables,

25

mad-houses, work-houses and houses of correction. At its endowment, the Empress gave each college 15,000 roubles and they were also heavily subsidised by donations from private individuals. The great merchant Demidov, for example, gave 20,000 roubles. In addition, in St Petersburg, Catherine donated a sum of 52,659 roubles originally intended to be used to erect a statue of herself. Some indication of how this money was utilised can be obtained by a glance at the Town Hospital at St Petersburg, which possessed 300 beds (though 400 could be housed in an emergency). The poor were admitted without payment. The patient was on admittance, shaved, bathed and put into a tidy dress. The beds were spaced well apart and had curtains which could be drawn around them. A professor of electricity was permanently employed by the hospital for the relief of those diseases in which he might be of service!

The St Petersburg House for Lunatics was renowned for the gentle treatment it meted out to patients who, when raving, were not chained but merely held by thongs to their beds. Only gentle remedies were applied, as, for example, strict diet!

The Empress was always very concerned with venereal diseases and built a fine hospital for sufferers 'destined [to quote Major Masson] for the reception of 50 ladies infected with a certain disease. No question is asked either as to the name or the quality of those who present themselves, and they are treated with equal care, respect and discretion. This last word is even marked on the linen appointed for their use.' All patients were gratuitously admitted but could not be discharged until they were completely cured—which shows exceptional foresight, particularly as prostitution was a well-developed trade at St Petersburg.

Catherine's attitude towards smallpox showed equal enlightenment. She was one of the first in Russia to submit to inoculation against the disease; in 1768 she summoned the Quaker, Dr Thomas Dimsdale, whose reputation in the practice of smallpox vaccination was of European renown, to perform the royal operation. The Senate was so impressed by her bravery in undergoing this ordeal and at the age of 40 into the bargain, that it bestowed 12 gold medals on her and put up an inscription in Senate House, stating: 'She saved others to the danger of herself.' How many others Catherine did actually save in her attempt to make smallpox vaccination general is difficult to ascertain. Despite her endowment of a Smallpox Hospital in 1768 for the more effectual

dissemination of inoculation, which twice a year admitted children free for this purpose, it would appear probable that immunisation only spread in any degree among the noble class. The peasants still preferred to run with their smallpox to the Virgin. As with her other efforts at education, Catherine only succeeded in carrying enlightenment to the most enlightened class.

Poster advocating smallpox vaccination

With her Foundling Hospital which she built on the banks of the Moskva, the Empress again broke new ground: it was one of the first establishments of its kind in Europe. She intended that it should, amongst other things, discourage infanticide. A branch was also endowed at St Petersburg in 1770, which served both as a lying-in hospital and a seminary of education. In the former capacity, it admitted all pregnant women who applied, without exception, enquiry or pay. In the latter, most of the children were educated as soon as possible in arts which would be of use to the state, to become tradesmen or mechanics, tailors or cobblers, in the case of the boys. The girls were first taught to make the different items of their own clothing and then moved on to higher things such as manufacturing fringes, lace and an exquisite embroidery used on court dresses, funeral palls and sacerdotal robes. The function of the Foundling Hospital has been described as the transformation of private indiscretion into national benefit.

Children of both sexes at the Foundling Hospital who showed some promise were sent to the Academy of Arts, the Gymnasium of the Academy of Sciences and the theatrical school. In 1779, the Petersburg Foundling Hospital sent 50 boys and girls for training in dramatic art with the famous actor Dmitrevsky. However, boys were discharged at the age of 24, girls at 20, free of all obligation. Mothers wishing their children to be accepted at the Foundling Hospital had only to ring the doorbell: a basket would be let down, the baby placed inside and the

The Grand Theatre at St Petersburg

basket retrieved. The mother was only asked to state the child's name and whether it had been baptised.

The theatrical school, mentioned above, took pupils of both sexes and instructed them in all the objects of the theatre: declamation, music, dancing, gesticulation and mimicry. The dearest ambition of its pupils was to perform at the Imperial Theatre, and many of them did indeed succeed in this. In 1780 to 1784 there were in fact four public theatres at St Petersburg, the Russian, the French, the German and the Italian opera, all heavily subsidised.

Apart from her support of the theatre, Catherine was always a great patron of the arts and of artists of all nationalities. In one year, for example, she set aside one million roubles for works of art. By the end of her reign, her collection of pictures could compete with that of any other European sovereign. She also made several valuable purchases for the Library of the Academy of Sciences, including in 1782 a collection made by an Englishman, Dr Fothergill, of animal and plant drawings by British artists (at a cost of £5,000). For the Museum of the Academy, her gifts included a collection of American curiosities, including 700 animals preserved in spirits, brought by a Swede, Colonel Dahlberg, from Surinam.

Her own private collections were not to be despised. Her library included three great purchases: the libraries of Voltaire, Diderot and Galliani; while her collection of natural history housed in the Imperial Museum at the Hermitage included the collection made by Professor Pallas and bought for 20,000 roubles. Her collection of antique works of art and jewels filled a large hall lined with cabinets, while that of copper-plate engravings contained over 30,000 prints by the greatest masters.

Catherine's services to the culture of her adopted country included the encouragement she gave to the study of the Russian language. In 1783 the Russian Academy was founded by the Princess Dashkov. It was devoted to the cultivation and determination of the Russian tongue. Three years later, Catherine appointed a yearly sum of 5,000 roubles for the Russian translations of books. Preference was to be given to Greek and Roman authors.

She also gave impetus, as we have seen, to the extended knowledge of the history and geography of Russia. In 1765, she sent an expedition to survey the country and its frontiers. It was instructed to pursue its enquiries on the different sorts of earths and waters; on the best methods of cultivating barren and desert spots; on local disorders incident to men and animals and the most efficacious means of relieving them; on breeding cattle, particularly sheep; on rearing bees and silkworms; on different places and objects for fishing and hunting; on minerals; on arts and trades; and on indigenous plants to form a *flora Russica*. The expedition was particularly instructed to rectify the longitudes and latitudes of the principal towns; to make astronomical, geographical and meteorological observations; to trace the courses of rivers; to take the most exact charts; to describe with accuracy the manners, customs, dresses, languages, antiquities, traditions, history and religions—in other words, to determine every item of information which could illustrate the real state of the Empire. Voyages of discovery were also undertaken for the promotion of geographical knowledge of the eastern and northern oceans.

She was no less assiduous in her research into Russian history. In 1779, she ordered the College of Foreign Affairs to make a collection of public treaties, both ancient and modern, under the direction of

Professor Muller of Moscow, the Keeper of the Archives of the College. Later she issued a command to the Synod to make a diligent search for old Russian manuscripts in its two libraries and ordered that the most ancient and most difficult should be rendered intelligible and transcribed and printed by competent people. A further command referred to the ransacking of all the libraries and monasteries throughout the Empire for chronicles and other manuscripts relating to the history of the country. Catherine herself set an example for the writing of history by publishing her own *Pieces relating to Russian History.*

Finally, despite her disregard of the system of bondage, Catherine was not indifferent to the economic state of Russia. She greatly helped the study of economics through the orders given to her governors for a continual census of the population, and by means of the table of vital statistics, prices and provisions, customs and duties, imports and exports etc., which she ordered to be made out and sent to the Academy of Sciences. Her most ambitious undertaking was the foundation, in 1765, of the Free Economic Society for the encouragement of agriculture and household management in Russia. Some of the main functions of the society were to take careful note of what went on in other countries and to disseminate information. A prize was offered annually for the best answer to a particular agricultural question. Copies of these treatises were even distributed to provincial libraries. In addition, questions and prizes were supplied by individual members. A look at but one such subject, set in this case by an anonymous member, gives some idea of the scope covered. 'Would it be more for the public good that the serf should possess land or that he should only be allowed to have movable property? How far should his rights to either extend?' Two years after the foundation of the society, Catherine herself offered 1,000 gold pieces for the best recommendations on how to organise an agricultural economy 'for the common good'. The society received 164 entries from all over Europe. The prize-winning essay came from France. In 1781 the society could boast 179 members, who met weekly to hear papers read. The Empress also sent several young men to Europe to study practical agriculture, several armed with recommendations to Arthur Young in England.

Thus, under this enlightened ruler, the knowledge of the country— its history, its geography, its statistics—increased, its museums were filled, its nobles were better educated, a language of its own came to life, literature and theatre revived and information on the possibilities of improving agriculture was accumulated—though not as yet very frequently employed. This is perhaps typical of all Catherine's grand schemes: the grandiose ideas which were never carried to complete realisation. The Comte de Ségur, the French Ambassador, sums it up:

'Catherine's imagination was never able to rest: moreover, her plans were more precipitous than mature; it was evident that this precipitation stifled at birth part of the creations of her genius. She wanted at one and the same time to form a third estate, attract foreign trade, establish manufactures, extend agriculture, found credit, increase paper money, raise the rate of exchange, lower the interest on money, build towns, create academies, people the deserts, cover the Black Sea with manifold squadrons, annihilate the Tartars, invade Persia, continue her progressive conquests of the Turks, enchain Poland and extend her influence over all Europe. This was a great deal to undertake and, although there was more to be done in a country so new to civilisation, it is certain that more success would have been obtained if fewer objects had been embraced at the same time.'

As it was, despite the fine ideas with which she had begun her reign, the condition of the serfs in bondage remained the same, or if anything, worsened, while Catherine herself lived amidst a court of unbelievable splendour. Isolated from the life of the country, a small hothouse plant growing on a bank of the rankest manure and nourished by it, Catherine held sway over one of the most extravagant and dazzling courts Russia had ever known. The extent of the isolation can be gauged from the Empress' amazing statement that in Russia 'every peasant has his turkey in the pot every Sunday', and that, 'though men died of over-eating, they never died of hunger'. The degree to which this isolation was encouraged can be seen in Potemkin's efforts to erect 'cardboard' villages to line Catherine's route on her grand expedition down the Dnieper to visit the Crimea. The Empress' glimpses of her country consisted of cleanly dressed, gaily waving peasants in national dress, forcibly imported with their flocks for the occasion, placed before attractive and hastily built model frame dwellings. When the Empress had passed, the peasants made their weary way home. Many, it is said, perished in the process.

Members of the court were equally capable of arranging similar exhibitions to impress foreigners. The Princess Dashkov writes as follows about her own attempt to show an English visitor the 'real' Russia:

'A village had been newly built on my estate ... and here I assembled all the peasants who were about to occupy it, dressed in their holiday suits, embroidered as is the custom with us by the females. The weather was delicious, and I encouraged them to dance on the grass, singing in accompaniment according to our country fashion.'

Potemkin showing Catherine an apparently prosperous village

For a view of the court we can scarcely do better than look through the eyes of a 14-year-old boy. The young Fonvizin wrote down his first impressions and his amazement at the splendour there: 'Everywhere glittering gold, an assembly of people in blue and red decoration ribbons, a multitude of fair women and finally an enormous orchestra.' An early traveller to the court in Catherine's reign confirmed his impressions: 'The opulence and pomp of the Russian Court exceeds all descriptions. An enormous suite of courtiers is constantly in attendance on the Empress.

(overleaf) *Peasants dancing*

Enlightened Despotism

Many of the grandees are virtually studded with diamonds; diamond buttons, diamonds on their shoe buckles and on the hilts of their swords.'

Contemporary accounts of a couple of celebrations give some indication of the magnificence of court life. Sir James Harris describes a fete given by the Empress on the occasion of the birth of her grandson, Alexander:

'The dessert at supper was set out with jewels to the amount of upwards of two millions sterling, and at the tables of Macao (a game much in vogue here at present) besides the stake in money played for, a diamond of fifty roubles value was given by her Imperial Majesty to each of those who got *nine*, the highest point of the game. One hundred and fifty diamonds were distributed in this manner. None but Russians of the highest rank were honoured with an invitation to this party, but for some days after, foreigners and others were admitted to a sight of this most beautiful decoration of jewels which was equally extraordinary for the elegance of the design, as for the costliness of the materials.'

Richardson describes a masquerade in the palace:

'Fourteen large rooms and galleries were opened for the accommodation of the masks; and I was informed that there were present several thousand people. A great part of the company wore dominos, or capuchin dresses. . . . The Empress herself, at the time I saw her Majesty, wore a Grecian habit, though I was afterwards told that she varied her dress two or three times during the masquerade. . . . At midnight, a spacious hall of a circular form, capable of containing a vast number of people and illuminated in the most magnificent manner, was suddenly opened. Twelve tables were placed in alcoves around the sides of the room, where the Empress, Prince Henry (of Prussia) and a hundred and fifty of the chief nobility and foreign ministers sat down to supper. The rest of the company went up by stairs on the outside of the room into the lofty galleries, placed all around on the inside. . . . The entertainment was enlivened with a concert of music and at different intervals, persons in various habits entered the hall and exhibited Cossack, Chinese, Polish, Swedish and Tartar dances. The whole was so gorgeous, and at the same time, so fantastic, that I could not help thinking myself present at some of the magnificent festivals described in the old fashioned romances. . . . The rest of the company, on returning to the rooms adjoining, found prepared for them also a sumptuous banquet. The masquerade began at six in the evening and continued till five next morning.

'Besides the masquerade, and other festivities, in honour of and to divert Prince Henry, we had lately a most magnificent show of fireworks. They were exhibited in a wide space before the Winter Palace, and in truth beggared description. They displayed by a variety of emblematical figures, the reduction of Moldavia, Wallachia, Bessarabia, and the various conquests and victories achieved since the commencement of the present war. The various colours, the bright green and the snowy white, exhibited in these fireworks, were truly astonishing. For the space of twenty minutes, a tree adorned with the loveliest and most verdant

Catherine with her favourite, Potemkin

foliage seemed to be waving as with a gentle breeze. It was entirely of fire: and during the whole of this stupendous scene, an arch of fire, by the continued throwing of rockets and fireballs in one direction, formed as it were a suitable canopy.'

To some, the stupendous round of gaiety that court life offered was just too exhausting for words. Guy Dickens commented: 'the good of the King's service requires that his Majesty should have at the Court a Minister in full strength and vigour of his age, as in their way of thinking here they look upon a Foreign Minister not missing a court day, masquerade, ball, play or any other public diversion, to be the chief and principal objects of his mission, which', he pathetically adds, 'at my

37

Catherine's portfolio case

time of life I cannot do.' Lord Cathcart also felt the social strain: 'Never having been a card-player, and having long ceased to be a dancer, I was obliged to decline the honour proposed to me of making the Empress's party.'

However, these criticisms of Catherine's court were mere superficialities. At greater depth, Sir James Harris reports:

'Great luxury and little morality seem to run through every rank. Flattery and servility characterize the inferior class, presumption and pride the higher one. A slight but brilliant varnish covers in both the most illiterate and uninformed minds. Their entertainments, their apartments and the number of their domestics, are quite Asiatic.'

Nor, as one might imagine from such a milieu were moral standards much observed. The Empress herself set the tone, taking throughout her years on the throne, right to the bitter end of her life, a series of lovers. They were publicly chosen, some even said vetted before choice by Dr Dimsdale and Countess Bruce, publicly acknowledged, heaped with the most costly gifts while in office and dismissed with equally costly presents when they had served their purpose. The office of lover to the Empress became almost a public position, filled in turn by Orlov, Poniatowski, Potemkin, Zavodovsky, Zoritch, Korsakov, Lanskey, and so on. . . . They were court officials, endowed with large salaries, honours, dignities and luxuriously appointed apartments close to Catherine's own. They even had their appointed place at table: at their royal mistress's right hand.

Catherine, in her private life, presented yet another paradox; she lived amidst all this splendour in a certain austerity. She was said to rise at five in the morning and be engaged in business until ten. She then breakfasted and went to prayers. She dined at two and then withdrew to her own apartment until tea at five. After tea she either saw company, played cards or went to a theatre, opera or masquerade until supper. She went to bed at ten and by eleven the palace was as quiet as the tomb. Whist was her favourite game of cards: she played skilfully and well and won often. She sometimes attended concerts but was not overfond of music. In the morning between prayers and dinner she frequently took an airing in coach or sledge, according to the season. On these occasions she sometimes had no guards and very few attendants, and did not choose to be known or saluted as Empress. Sir John Harris even records that on several occasions he supped frugally alone with Catherine off a card table without attendants or spectators. She was fond of small dinner parties of eight or ten persons and she frequently supped, went to balls or masquerades in the houses of her nobility. When she retired to her palaces in the country, especially Tsarskoe Selo, she laid aside all state and lived with her ladies on a footing of as easy intimacy as possible. Any one of them who rose when she entered the room was fined a rouble and all these fines were given to the poor. In fact, the first rule in her *Regulations to which all who enter therein must submit* was: 'They will leave their dignity at the door together with their hats and swords.'

2   The Western Capital of Western Culture

The brilliant pageant of court life unfurled against the no less brilliant background of St Petersburg. It was a St Petersburg of relatively recent foundation, which had been built during the lifetime of some of Catherine's subjects. They had seen the first small house that Peter had erected for himself transformed into the magnificent city created for the Empress Elizabeth by her Italian architect, Rastrelli. Catherine, aided by the Scottish architect, Charles Cameron, embellished the city in classical style.

Rastrelli it was who had built the Winter Palace which formed the setting for some of Catherine's most elaborate entertainments. Standing on the site of Peter's original palace of the same name facing the Neva, it had a rococo front and was surrounded by gardens and pavilions. But its 1,500 rooms were not enough for Catherine. Lover of the 'simple' life and convert to Jean-Jacques Rousseau's fashion for hermitages, she ordered three extra buildings to be erected, one by the French architect Vallin de la Mothe, a second by a Russian, Veldten, a third by Quarenghi. Known respectively as the first Hermitage, the Old Hermitage and the Hermitage Theatre, these buildings were all connected by covered galleries to the Winter Palace and, as it were, formed a temple raised to social recreation and unconstrained amusement.

One of the buildings housed the pictures and many *objets d'art* which Catherine had been steadily adding to the collections of her predecessors. It contained the Empress' private library and her picture gallery, where she displayed works by Raphael, Guido Reni, Tiepolo, Titian, Van Dyck, Rembrandt, Rubens and others—for the Empress kept a vigilant eye on all the important sales in Europe. Here also was Raphael's gallery, an exact copy of that in the Vatican, as well as a great collection of prints, medals, coins, minerology and natural history, a variety of ingenious models, and a dazzling display of antique and modern gems. Dispersed around the walls, contemplating these treasures, were the busts of great men of the past. Other apartments in the Hermitage were devoted to musical entertainment; yet others to billiards, while one of the courtyards was formed into a pleasure garden heated in winter and covered with a fine wire netting. Here beautiful and rare birds flew in and out the trees and bushes or squabbled for the crumbs the Empress threw them. Another covered way led to the court theatre built by Quarenghi in 1780 on a round plan. Its exterior was decorated with columns and colossal statues of Greek, Roman and Russian dramatists. The hall for spectators formed a series of semi-circular steps, gradually growing narrower, covered

Walking in the gardens of Peter's Summer Palace

with cloth and each with its individual cushion. From its seats, the Empress would watch both professional and amateur productions, in which prominent nobles participated.

The Marble Palace was an example of the classical architecture modelled on the Greek and Roman styles then much in vogue in western Europe. Designed by Antonio Rinaldi for Gregory Orlov, it formed a gigantic oblong pile on the banks of the Neva. Its towers reared proudly aloft. It was three storeys high, the lowest granite, the superstructure grey Siberian marble decorated with columns and pilasters of reddish marble. Though the building was of classical simplicity, the window-frames were of cast brass highly gilt, and the balconies on the two sides had balustrades of brass gilt. The roof rested on iron bars and was covered with sheet copper.

The Tauridian Palace, once belonging to Potemkin, was converted by Catherine into her Autumn Palace at enormous expense and in a great hurry. No less than 1,500 men were employed on the scheme. They even worked at night by the light of torches. Their achievement was of corresponding grandeur. A vast quadrangular vestibule, lit by the windows

Tsarskoe Selo

of the second storey, was surrounded by a gallery for the orchestra and furnished with an organ. From there, a double row of pillars led to the main saloon, some hundred paces long with a double colonnade of colossal pillars; boxes for the company between the columns were decorated with silk curtains and festoons. Lustres of cut glass hung from the ceiling and their light was reflected by two enormous mirrors. A winter garden was built along one side of the room, its heat maintained by fires concealed in the walls and pillars; lead pipes filled with boiling water even ran under the earth. The garden itself was embellished with statues, a grotto of looking-glasses, an obelisk of mirrors and numerous other wonders.

Nor did Catherine confine her architectural activities to the secular. On a site occupied since the foundation of the city by a small wooden church, the Isaac Church, Catherine planned to build a cathedral. When she died the church was still unfinished, though building had been in progress for 26 years. Yet she may have lived to see the lowest floor of granite rise from the ground and the completion of its marble, jasper and porphyry superstructure, even perhaps the beginning of the dome.

So far we have wandered at random around the city centre of St Petersburg, but other centres of court festivity could be reached by following the road to the south out of the city. Here lay the summer palaces of the nobility—hardly less ostentatious, each standing in its individual and finely planned gardens, parks and shrubberies. (These, incidentally, were opened for inspection by suitably garbed members of the public at specific times and furnished many a 'respectable' family with a fine afternoon's entertainment.) Not the least notable was the Empress' own palace at Tsarskoe Selo. The first palace there had been built by Peter for his second wife Catherine I, but Rastrelli, under Elizabeth's direction, effected a total reconstruction, while Cameron under Catherine II further enhanced its beauty.

The effect of Rastrelli's Great Palace was truly magnificent. A low semi-circle of out-buildings and servants' quarters, broken by three wrought-iron gates, swept in front of the main palace, three storeys high and 326 feet long. One of the Empress Catherine's favourite rooms within the vast interior was the Amber Room, where many of her small concerts, games and evening parties took place. The walls were overlaid

Elevation of window wall, Lyons drawing room, Tsarskoe Selo

The enfilade of doorways at Tsarskoe Selo

with light, transparent, honey-coloured amber, topped with a painted mock-amber frieze and fitted with elaborate gilded bronze ornaments, mirrors and pilasters of looking-glass. The ceiling bore a painting by an Italian artist *The Triumph of Wisdom over Voluptuousness*. Even more wondrous was the Great Hall, 52 feet broad and two storeys high. It was lit in the daytime by 13 pairs of double windows on two sides of the room, the spaces between them panelled by mirrors in rococo gilded frames. At night 696 lights sparkled their reflections into the mirrors.

These were but two of the hundreds of rooms in this superb ensemble. Catherine, needless to say, had her own changes to make to Elizabeth's model. Cameron made for her the Salon de Lyons with richly inlaid parquetry floor, fireplace and table of lapis lazuli and walls and furniture upholstered in yellow Lyons silk woven with branches and little birds. Apart from several other small state

44

Monbijou in the park of Tsarskoe Selo

apartments, he was responsible for a series of private rooms, including the Silver Cabinet, where she spent many of her working hours. Her bedroom had walls inlaid with medallions of Wedgwood porcelain, and contained columns of purple glass with bronze bases and capitals. Her boudoir—she called it her 'Snuff Box'—held an enormous couch built into the whole width of the small room, panelled with opalescent white glass and gilded ornaments, its door framed in columns of blue glass.

No less remarkable than the interior of Tsarskoe were its gardens, filled with varied and magnificent park-buildings. To those already in existence, Catherine added the Agate Pavilion, again built by Cameron. It consisted of three rooms: a central salon and two adjoining apartments, with walls of solid jasper interspersed with red agate overlaid with medallions and bronze reliefs. There were marble fireplaces and huge chandeliers shaped like women, with branches of gilded bronze.

These were but a few of the buildings which formed the setting of St Petersburg court life. They have been chosen as they illustrate the luxury, the artistic fashion and the vast scale on which the passion for pleasure was indulged.

Catherine's choice of St Petersburg as her capital city—as opposed to the traditional capital of old Muscovy, Moscow—emphasised the link between herself and her illustrious predecessor, Peter the Great. Two examples of this emphasis should suffice. Peter, when he founded the city, had built himself a small one-storey house of logs in Dutch style, painted to look like brick and roofed with shingles. It was about 60 feet long, by 20 broad, and contained only two rooms and a kitchen. In 1784, Catherine enclosed this house within a stone building to protect it from the weather and preserve it as a historical monument. Catherine then erected a bronze statue of the founder by Falconet, bearing the inscription PETRO PRIMO CATHERINA SECUNDA. The statue, standing on an immense granite rock, depicts the founder, clad in Russian dress, seated on his horse and stretching out an arm in a gesture of parental affection for his people. The horse shown ascending the rock-like base rears wildly as it tramples on an enormous coiling snake, interpreted by some as representing Envy.

To appreciate the significance of Catherine's choice of St Petersburg, it is necessary to understand the reasons which had led Peter to build this city. It was no obvious site. The town was constructed on the

Erection of the statue of Peter the Great

St Petersburg in 1753

swampy delta and islands at the mouth of the Neva river, where buildings had to be entirely erected on piles driven into the marshy ground.
The river was icebound from November to March and the climate was
appalling. Over a period of ten years, it was calculated that St Petersburg annually enjoyed a total of 97 bright days, 104 of rain, 72 of
snow and 93 unsettled. The shortest day had only five and a half hours
of daylight. Terrible floods inundated the city when the river broke its
banks. Finally, an unhealthy mist rose from the marshes, spreading
disease and pestilence. But St Petersburg faced west and it was as a
western city which would encourage trade and intercourse with the
West that Peter had conceived it.

Building St Petersburg was no easy matter. Forced labour had to be
imported and thousands of lives were lost from disease. Populating it
was no easier. Here again, force was necessary and many were the
ukazi that required specific numbers of noble or merchant families to
build houses on the banks of the Neva, or that prohibited the erection
of new buildings at Moscow in the hope that energies and material
would be diverted to the rival capital. The haste with which the city
grew and the circumstances surrounding its growth led Count Algarotti
to remark that 'their walls are all cracked out of perpendicular and ready
to fall. It has been wittily enough said that ruins make themselves in
other places, but that they were built at Petersburg.'

Tradition drew the population to the old capital at Moscow and

47

(overleaf) *View of St Petersburg and the River Neva*

economic considerations also acted in Moscow's favour. St Petersburg was at a great distance from most of the large noble estates, far also from easily available supplies of foodstuffs. If the noble lived at Moscow, he could live easily and cheaply off his estate. At St Petersburg, most of his provisions—not only luxury items but the simplest necessities, even timber for fuel—had to be bought from a retailer and, as they had been transported over great distances, at high prices. Additional expense was incurred by the huge cost that was involved in maintaining his palace there amid the rigours of the climate and the unsuitability of the site. This was disastrous for the poorer members of the noble class, particularly as they had previously been able to spend a good part of the year living on their estates and commuting to Moscow to fulfil their service obligations.

The nobles, however, gradually came to accept St Petersburg. The more conservative merchant class retained its loyalty to Moscow and many of them kept their houses there, encouraged in this by the freezing of the Neva during the long winter which put an end to sea trade. But the distance of St Petersburg from the country as a whole engendered a new attitude amongst the nobles who lived there. They came to regard the court as their sole fatherland, while the very remoteness of the city kept the sighs of the people and the hardships of their villages from reaching their ears.

Washerwomen in the neighbourhood of St Petersburg

No real corporate life had developed in St Petersburg at this period, partly because the nobles tended to move out to their country houses on the outskirts of the city at the approach of summer; partly, too, because of the constant flow of the lower classes in and out of St Petersburg. Throughout the summer, many thousands arrived to

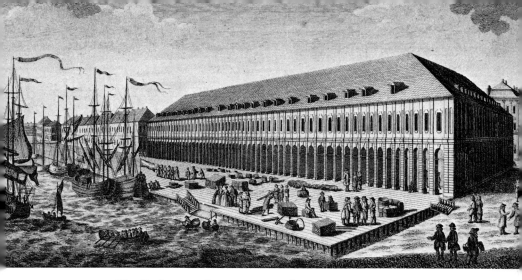

The Exchange and warehouses at St Petersburg

work as carpenters, bricklayers, masons, house-painters and so on, on the vast building projects. They would return home to their land at the beginning of winter, to be replaced by other peasants prepared to seek employment as ice-cutters. Few of these workers owned permanent residences or property in St Petersburg. They often did not even leave their place of work in the evening and slept on the building site or on the barks which brought the timber up the Neva, even in the cellars of large houses or in half-built rooms of unfinished constructions.

Peter had planned St Petersburg as a German-Dutch city; under Elizabeth it gained a Franco-Italian rococo elegance. By the last decade of the eighteenth century, it was a city of glitter, opulence, luxury, art and elegance, with an estimated population of 218,000 as compared with 74,000 in 1750. These included a large proportion of foreigners— one-seventh of the total population of the city, according to one estimate. But the lower classes who drifted in and out of the city on seasonal labour were not included in these statistics. It had been transformed from an imitation Dutch naval base to a stately granite capital. Catherine, it was said, received a Petersburg of wood and left it of brick. It became a city of straight, broad, long streets, frequently intersecting in abrupt, sharp corners, spacious open squares and numerous canals. The variety in the architecture of the houses and the beautiful River Neva with its substantial and elegant embankments made the general view brilliant and enchanting. Even at this stage, however, St Petersburg was still developing.

51

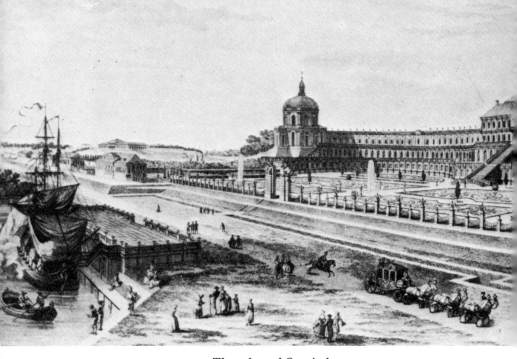

The palace of Oranienbaum

Large waste spots would be noted one year and covered with houses the next. A traveller returning after an absence of but a few years would find himself totally lost, so great and so rapid were the changes. The magnificent Fontanka Canal had only recently been a muddy streamlet with miserable wooden huts along its banks.

Peter had founded this city to increase trade with the West. That his foresight was justified is amply testified by the number of vessels using the quays on the riverside. According to the St Petersburg academician Dr Johann Gottlieb Georgi, they rose from 100 to 200 before 1750 to 900–1,000 in 1788. These statistics, however rough they may be, do at least indicate a steady rise in trade with the West, and particularly with England and Holland. He had also intended to establish a capital city which should be truly a western capital. He realised that if Russia were to take its place amongst the western powers, a western façade was indispensable. Only when this had been supplied could full contact on an equal basis be established with western Europe. It was necessary to

convey to the foreigner living in the capital, the illusion of living in the most civilised of cities, the most cultured of courts and in an advanced and educated country. St Petersburg was to be the showplace of Russian westernisation.

There is no doubt that this was assisted by the large number of foreigners resident in St Petersburg and most of these came from the West. The largest colony was made up of Germans (Peter the Great had encouraged the Russo-German flow) but Britons came a good second in the size of their community and the importance of its contribution to the life of the city. There was, firstly, an important group of British merchants who possessed their own, officially recognised, business houses and places on the quays. Secondly, a considerable number of both English and Scots served in the Russian Admiralty, in ranks ranging from admirals (such as Greig and Elphinstone) to naval engineers (such as Sir Samuel Bentham), down to ordinary seamen and naval workers. They were also well represented in the professions and

View of Moscow from the Kremlin looking towards the Moscowa Bridge

trades. There had been English and Scottish doctors, working in Russia since at least the end of the sixteenth century—by the middle of the seventeenth there was said to be no town of any size in the Empire without one. In 1766, Dr John Rogerson of Dumfries was appointed Court Physician to the Empress Catherine, and in 1768, Dr Thomas Dimsdale, the Quaker, was summoned to exercise his skill in smallpox vaccination. In St Petersburg during the same period were also the engraver, James Walker, a pupil of Valentine Green, a certain Mr Jackson, who made musical instruments, and one Morgan who sold mathematical instruments. There were also English tailors (who often specialised in riding-clothes) and gardeners, such as Bush and Gould. From France and Italy came architects, musicians, actors and painters and from Austria, at least one woman of note—a well-known riding mistress, Nanette Mahueu.

It was also desirable that the Russian travelling abroad should appear as a civilised member of the European community. Only too frequently in the past, the Russian noble had seemed like a being from another planet, or at least another continent, when he visited a western court. He was, according to John Mottley in 1744 'distinguished among Foreigners by the grossness of his manners'. Peter himself, when he travelled in England in 1698, shocked by the barbarity of his conduct. Sir Christopher Wren assessed the damage caused by his retinue at the house where they stayed at £350 9s. 6d. Glass was broken, some 60 chairs lost or dirtied, several doors cut up, and feather beds, sheets, curtains and silk counterpanes ripped.

Peter, however, profited from his experiences abroad. On his return, he initiated his policy of turning the Asiatic Russian noble into a western aristocrat. Beards were forcibly shaved; the flowing sleeves of the old Asiatic garments cut off and European dress made *de rigueur*; the ladies were drawn out of their Asiatic seclusion; he imported a host of foreign artists and engineers from Europe and in turn encouraged Russian youth to travel to acquire foreign ideas. And finally he founded St Petersburg, which came to be regarded as the symbol of all that was western in Russian life: French fashions and Prussian uniforms, Italian architects and English gardeners, European trade and European culture.

By identifying herself with the founder of the city and by establishing

Moscow, showing the Square and main shops

her capital and her court at Petersburg, Catherine was pledging herself to continue this policy. In its negative aspect, it meant the abandonment of Moscow, the old Asiatic capital of the Empire. Its positive aspect implied the continued and rapid westernisation of the country. Catherine wrote of Moscow: 'The town is full of symbols of fanaticism, churches, miraculous icons, priests and convents. . . .' 'Never', she wrote elsewhere, 'had a people before its eyes more objects of fanaticism, more wonder-working images . . . more churches, more of the clerical crew, more convents, more devout hypocrites, more beggars, more thieves. . . .' The population there, she felt, was ready at the slightest provocation to oppose law and order. In St Petersburg however, 'the inhabitants are more docile and polite, less superstitious, more accustomed to foreigners, from contact with whom they always acquire something valuable'.

In point of fact, Catherine's reign witnessed an unprecedented influx of foreign fashions in thought, letters, instruction and social intercourse, to which the Empress herself gave every stimulus. She delighted in French ideas and, as we have already mentioned, did much to disseminate them throughout the country. She was a great admirer of Voltaire, and corresponded with him from 1763 until his death in 1778. She then bought his books for her library and ordered a definitive edition of his work, 'so that I can distribute them everywhere. I want people to study them, to learn them by heart, to feed their souls on them. This will develop citizens, men of genius, heroes and authors: it

57

(overleaf) Moscow, showing two extremes of poverty and wealth

will bring forth a hundred thousand talents which might otherwise be lost in the dark night of ignorance.' Diderot was another of her illustrious correspondents and once again, when he was in need, she bought his library and, allowing it to remain in his possession, paid him an annual salary of 1,000 francs as librarian to look after it. Similarly, she offered to publish d'Alembert's encyclopaedia in Russia when its progress in France was endangered. At Diderot's instigation, many learned men, including Grimm, most Frenchified of Germans, came from France to the Russian court. From 1764 onwards, Catherine paid a subscription of 1,500 roubles a year for Grimm's newsletter, *Correspondance Littéraire*, which he sent to most German and some foreign courts. Later Grimm became one of her most constant correspondents and closest friends.

'Franco-mania' proved highly infectious. It spread through the Russian court and by contagion reached the nobility. To be French was to be European. To be European was to touch the heights of culture and civilisation.

Almost everything was written in French and it was in that language that the classics of Greece and Rome, as well as those of England and Germany reached Russia. A corresponding movement drove Russian writers to translate Molière and Racine, Corneille, La Fontaine, Montesquieu and Voltaire into Russian, as well as to compose works of their own in imitation. The acquisition of French culture became a status symbol. Sometimes the nobleman took a genuine interest in the literature of western Europe, or at least of France, and shared the literary ideas and judgements current in the West. According to the Comte de Ségur, the women outstripped the men in this cultural advance:

'You could already find a large number of elegant ladies, young girls remarkable for their accomplishments, speaking seven or eight languages equally well, playing several instruments and familiar with the work of the most famous French, English and Italian poets and novelists.'

French became the language of the Russian court. Russian was reserved for the use of servants and often spoken very badly. Martha Wilmot tells of an Englishwoman married to a Russian who voiced the hope of learning the language of her new land. Her husband's reply was that 'it would be totally useless except to speak to the servants'. Those unversed in the French tongue approximated to the dizzy social

A letter in French from Catherine to the Grand Duke Paul

heights by intermingling foreign words with their native Russian. This social snobbery is exemplified in the eighteenth-century guide for the good conduct of young gentlemen. It bade them converse in a foreign language, especially in the presence of servants, so that they might

La Harpe, tutor to Catherine's grandson, Alexander

be distinguished from ignorant dolts. Princess Dashkov sadly writes in her memoirs that 'according to the opinions of the time, we had the best of educations. We were instructed in four different languages and spoke French fluently. . . . The result, that I spoke Russian very imperfectly was hardly surprising.' Karamzin in 1790, when travelling in Europe, was deeply impressed by the fact that educated Englishmen preferred their own language, quite unlike his countrymen, who would rather speak French badly than talk to each other in Russian. In surprise, he comments: 'Even though all well-bred Englishwomen know French, they will not speak it. . . .'

Everything European was thought to be good and it was fashionable to employ European tutors. Catherine engaged M. La Harpe (a Free Swiss) to educate her grandchildren Alexander and Constantine. But not all imported tutors were of this calibre. Novikov wrote that the French ships brought to Russian ports not only trifles, but triflers, and swindlers as well, the whole brood of French adventurers who called themselves barons, chevaliers, marquises and counts, people whose main qualifications for teaching Russian youth were their quarrels with the Paris police. Other examples of misplaced confidence abound: a wealthy family near Moscow kept a Swede in the firm belief that his native language was German; another, a Finn who for years taught his own language in place of French to an eager Muscovite Francophil; a shady Spanish adventurer, good for little more than fencing and bragging of his experiences in countries he had never seen, was employed by a nobleman to prepare his sons for Moscow University. Radishchev's Frenchman, soldier of fortune and hairdresser, managed to hold down a job as a tutor for over a year until his employers discovered he could not read. Finally, there was the tutor who excused his lack of familiarity with the moods of French verbs by explaining that he had not been in Paris for some time and that 'the modes' there changed very frequently.

French fashion in dress and social convention penetrated even more rapidly; it was no longer thought seemly in the best circles to spit on the floor in public, pick the lice from your scalp (except in the privacy of the bed-chamber), eat with your fingers or beat your wife to a jelly. But emulation was not confined to such basic elements of behaviour. Macartney considered it went to quite absurd lengths.

'In France it is the etiquette of fashion to begin the Spring Season at Easter and to mark it by dress; the imitative Russian does the same and flings off his winter garments whilst the earth is covered with snow and themselves shivering with cold. It is the peculiar privilege of the noblesse of Paris to have Swiss porters at the gates of their hotels. At Petersburg a Russ gentleman of any fashion must have a Swiss also, or some tall fellow with a lace belt and hanger which it seems are indispensable accoutrements of a Parisian janitor.'

Westernisation had taken place so quickly that it is not surprising that western habits and customs were on the whole restricted to externals and that behind the façade lay deserts of ignorance. English visitors to the court comment time and time again on this anomaly. Listen to Martha Wilmot:

'Instead therefore of the dignified Salutation of former times (namely of bowing seriously to one another till their Crowns met together) you are Kissed on both your cheeks with the appearance of transport and are told mechanically how enchanted they are to make your acquaintance etc. The dress too is a bad imitation of the French and they have universally adopted their language. . . . They can't eat their dinners without a French cook to dress it, and can't educate their children without unprincipled adventurers from Paris to act as Tutors and Governesses. Every House of consequence has an outcast Frenchman to instruct the Heir apparent—in a word, when every association of fashion, luxury, elegance and fascination is drawn from France . . . the national music, the national dancing, the national Salutation, the national dress and the national language have all sunk down to the Ground and none but Slaves practice any! What I have seen therefore has been a superstructure from France—the Monkey rampant on the Bear's back.'

Elsewhere she aptly compares the imperial realm to a 'clumsy ignorant girl of 12 years old with a fine Parisian cap upon her head'. Or again:

'The land is overrun with French as with locusts. Milliners to the amount of some hundreds sell off ends of Gauze etc. at the most exorbitant prices because they pretend they are just arrived from Paris tho 'tis known half their goods come from Russian shops at the other end of the Town; and still they talk and cajole and make fortunes from the pockets of those who allow themselves to be duped and deserve it from their blind devotion to the Magic of the Word *Paris*. Dancing masters are of course French, so are multitudes of Physicians. In short, profession and trade of the domestic kind (I mean tailors, Mantua-makers, Milliners, Waiting Maids, Cooks, Book-sellers etc.) swarm with French.'

A contemporary English traveller, A. Swinton wrote:

'Russia resembles an heir newly come to his estate. She is only beginning to learn and seems struck at her own importance. This young heir has got his different masters to attend him: the English master is teaching him the art of navigation and commerce; the French, as usual, to dance and to dress; the Italian is drawing plans for his house and teaching him to sing; the German makes him wheel to the right and left, and teaches him all the other arts of war.'

And again:

'The truth is the Russians are going too fast in affecting, as well as attaining improvement. Foreigners have put too many things into their heads and, I believe, are picking their pockets, by the idle schemes with which they amuse them. The Russians in general look upon foreigners as a kind of superior being in regard to the arts and sciences.'

The comments of two English visitors on the architectural features of the city, neatly sum up the character of St Petersburg in the second half of the eighteenth century: Sir N. Wraxall regarded it as 'only an immense outline, which will require further empresses and almost future ages to complete'; while R. Johnston commented: 'Everything as it were in outline, nothing perfect, nothing to please; everything to astonish; a mixture of splendid barbarism and mighty rudeness.'

One consequence, however, of this embracing of western culture had more deep-reaching effects: the gap between the bonded peasant laboriously grinding out his life in the fields of the immense Russian countryside and the Europeanised French-speaking noble isolated in the far-off palaces of Petersburg became unbridgeable.

3   The Nobility

The landowning gentry—the noble class—was by far the most influential factor in Russian life in the second half of the eighteenth century. During the reign of Catherine the Great, it reached a pinnacle of unprecedented power. It made up only a comparatively small proportion of the total population: there were some half a million nobles in Russia in the 1760s out of a total population of 28 million. But they alone possessed two vital attributes: the right to own land, and the right to own serfs.

Several features peculiar to Russia differentiated this class from its western counterpart. Besides the fundamental difference which the right of ownership over their fellow humans constituted, there was also the fact that membership of the noble class in Russia depended not on birth, as in the West, but on service. This linking of the concept of service with the institution of serfdom dated back to the reign of Peter the Great, when the idea of a state to which all members owed service was developed. The noble served the state by entering the standing army, navy, civil administration or court officialdom; the serf served it by cultivating the soil. All members of the upper classes were compelled to give this form of service in one or other of the categories mentioned. Peter's famous Table of Ranks was an integral part of this scheme. Here, for example, Grade 1 comprised the rank of Field Marshal or Chancellor, Grade 2 Full General or Privy Councillor and so on down to Grade 13, Second Lieutenant or Senatorial Registrar and Grade 14 Ensign (or Cornet) or Collegiate Registrar. Any man, however humble his origin, could enter the service, climb through the grades and, if and when he attained the top eight, become a member of the nobility with the concomitant privileges of owning serfs, land and exemption from capitation tax. The fact that ancestry was of no account in the service and that a man of the most humble origin could become a field marshal is particularly important in understanding the character of the Russian noble class.

However, even during the reign of Peter the Great, many nobles had succeeded in evading the obligation to serve, though they retained the privileges of owning serfs and land. Under Peter III and Catherine, this position was legalised—though it must be stated that, in actuality, even after they were freed from legal obligation, only invalid or extremely poor nobles failed to spend a good part of their active lives in the service. The charm of the gay life in St Petersburg and the spur of ambition prompted the majority to continue to serve. Their absence from their estates on service was largely responsible for the growing alienation between master and serf.

This absenteeism can also be blamed to a large extent for the low productivity of the Russian soil and the slow adoption of improved methods of agriculture. Although newly founded journals in the second half of the eighteenth century began to publish hundreds of articles on agricultural subjects, with the main purpose of suggesting ways of increasing production; although some enlightened landlords at that period established societies for the promotion of agriculture (including the Free Economic Society); although the government made spasmodic attempts to raise the level of agricultural production and introduce new crops (in 1763, the English Ambassador to Moscow reported that 'every method had been taken in the Ukraine to advance and improve the cultivation of tobacco. Books of instruction are printed and distributed, a bounty promised to those who produce such a quantity and plants are sent from England'); despite all these attempts, the noble generally was loath to make the effort to introduce the new methods. To him, the land, as well as those who worked it for him, was merely there to be utilised, to support him in the luxury in which he wished to live. Great truck-loads of farm produce moved continuously from the country estates to the great city mansions. Very little thought was given to production for the market as opposed to production for consumption. In fact, even by the end of the century, it has been estimated that only 20 per cent of total grain production was sold on the market by the producers and only about one per cent exported.

The landlord's absence on service also explains another of the major differences between the Russian and western noble: the former had none of the strong attachments to his own family estate that were to be found in the West. He sold, exchanged or abandoned it with ease and moved his family elsewhere to farm greener, more productive pastures.

A Russian soldier and his officer

This lack of roots explains the nobleman's detachment from the soil and from his peasants, and the ease with which he could adapt himself to capital cities and foreign lands.

True, most members of the nobility towards the middle of the eighteenth century were born on their fathers' estates and spent their early years on the land, though the winter months were frequently passed in the city. But the father was absent for long periods on service and could not visit his family or estate very regularly—in fact, he sometimes stayed away for years at a time. Some nobles took their families with them when they travelled away from home to fulfil their service obligation. Even so, the sense of permanence was lacking, and service needs in any case made these moves fairly frequent. Even residence in the town meant separation from the larger family unit and estate.

Schooling did nothing to tighten the bond between the noble and his land. Education for the nobility had been compulsory since the time of Peter the Great. Towards the middle of the century, a minority of wealthier families were following the practice of inviting private tutors to live on their estates and teach their children but, though this practice grew, school was still the most commonly accepted method. A typical example was the Land Cadet Corps College, restored by the Empress in

1766. It was a military school where the child entered at the age of five or six and stayed for 15 years. To gain admittance, two requisites had to be satisfied: the boy's father had to be a noble; the child himself had to enjoy perfect health. On reception, the boy was placed in the first class and dressed in a brown sailor's jacket with a blue sash. He was cared for by women—a directress and ten *gouvernantes* were employed. Three years later he moved to the second class, donned a blue jacket and passed on to instruction by eight governors and an inspector. In another three years, his jacket changed to grey and his supervisors to field officers: this was the third class. By the time he reached the fourth class or First Military Age, he was wearing full uniform and his training had become the responsibility of the officers of the Corps.

The system was calculated to harden the constitution of the pupil. In the severity of winter, no cloak was permitted. The food was simple, though well prepared. Meat was served once a day at noon; breakfast was a roll; tea a slice of black bread; and supper boiled fruit and vegetables. The drink was water. The spacious dormitories, in which each age group slept, were barely heated and each cadet had anyway to quit his individual bed at five in the morning. The next two hours were spent at his ablutions and breakfast. Then from seven till eleven he sat at his school books. An hour before lunch was devoted to bodily exercise, but instruction was resumed at two and continued till five. The hours between five and seven were set aside for recreation followed by supper. By nine o'clock, all the cadets, regardless of age, were in bed.

Cleanliness at this establishment was carried to a high degree and moral welfare was safeguarded by continual inspections by governors and officers. Corporal punishment was prohibited. The pupil was seldom—and then only with the special permission of the chief, never without an attendant, and only for a few hours on a Sunday—allowed to leave the school and visit his parents and relations. However, there was no restriction on the visits they might receive at the Corps.

Besides the general elements of grammar and religion, the pupils were taught the Russian, German and French languages, geography, statistics, history, natural philosophy, belles-lettres, logic, civil and military architecture, geometry and algebra. Lessons were also given in drawing, dancing, riding, fencing, vaulting, turning in wood and ivory, recitation and declamation, and measurement and land-surveying. Most of these classes were not conducted in the Russian tongue.

The atmosphere of this school and others like it, where the formative years were spent, was very remote from the life of the country as a whole and even from that of the family estate. Boys were sent away at ages varying from six and seven to 12–13. Schools were few, the distances great, transport difficult and families were often on the move; as a result the noble son was often separated from his family throughout the year and sometimes for several years at a stretch. The strong camaraderie which developed in the schools gradually replaced his distant family in the child's life and placed a barrier between him and those who had not shared the experience with him. The barrier was heightened by the schools' policy of counteracting the barbarous home atmosphere their pupils had imbibed. They aimed consciously at producing a new 'civilised' race, and the education they dispensed was westernised and had no connection with pre-Petrine Russia. The old Russian history and literature were barely mentioned, the Russian language was largely neglected and, as we have seen, rarely used even to give lessons.

A vicious circle was thus in operation: the Russian nobility was already separated from the other sections of society by its greater degree of education and more sophisticated style of life: the schooling it received consciously widened the gulf between the educated élite and the people. The importance of education as a criterion of nobility can be seen in the fact that the very poor noblemen, who could not afford this luxury, were hardly considered nobility and became assimilated into the ranks of the peasantry. Furthermore, it bred an ignorance of the realities of Russia and an acceptance of western philosophical, aesthetic and cultural criteria in all spheres of life.

The Russian nobleman's right to own serfs was, as already mentioned, the major factor distinguishing him from the western squire. As it acquired the superficial veneer of western sophistication, the Russian nobility quickly realised the advantages to be gained from absolute power over its fellow men. The Russian gentleman was able to employ at least six times as many servants for his personal service as people of the same rank in western Europe. The domestic staff of a great Russian lord could number several hundred and a less wealthy man a minimum of 20. And

70

these servants cost the master nothing, except the price of their food and training, and he had no obligations towards them.

The letters and memoirs of the time constantly refer to the innumerable domestics: ' . . . if they have one livery servant they have seven and twenty, besides others that flit by at every turn. At the door of each apartment sits a servant to save me the trouble of opening or shutting the door . . .', writes Martha Wilmot. Elsewhere she comments:

'the number of servants is dreadful. Think of two, three and often four hundred servants to attend a small family. A Russian Lady scorns to use her own feet to go upstairs, and I do not Romance when I assure you that two powder'd footmen support her [Princess Dashkov's] lily white elbows and nearly lift her from the ground, a couple more follow with all manner of shawls, Pelises, etc. There is not a Bell in Russia except to the Churches, but if a fair-one gently calls, four or five footmen are ready in any antechambers to obey her summons. . . .'

The great lord had his own butlers, carpenters, goldsmiths and ebony workers, as well as cooks, valets and grooms. Some even had their own regiments complete with serfs dressed as soldiers and trained to carry out parades and mock battles. In addition, the Russian nobles were great lovers of spectacle and often had their own theatrical companies, orchestras and ballets. Many of their palaces were equipped with their own theatres, where the serfs could perform for the guests' pleasure in the evenings. 'Our labourers, our cooks, our footmen, and *femmes de Chambre* turn into Princes, Princesses, Shepherds and Shepherdesses', writes Miss Wilmot, 'and perform with a degree of spirit that is astonishing. 'Tis droll enough to be attended at Supper by the Hero of the piece who has been strutting before your Eyes in Gilded robes etc. for half the Evening.'

The owners' differing tastes were reflected in the companies they maintained. Prince N. B. Yusupov, who owned 21,421 serfs in 15 provinces, used to invite his intimate friends to performances by his serf *corps de ballet*. At a signal from the master, the girls would slip off their dresses and appear naked before the audiences. On the other hand, N. I. Shakhovskoy of Ardatov scrupulously watched over his company's morality. The house in which the actors lived was divided into separate

A Russian concert

dormitories for men and women and contact between the two was forbidden on the penalty of severe corporal punishment. An example of one such punishment is the 'spiked collar': the guilty party was placed in the centre of a room with his neck propped up by three poles. A special punishment designed for musicians consisted of a chain to which a dog-collar was fastened. Shakhovskoy's actors were not allowed to touch his actresses even during the performance, but ordered to stand at a distance of at least one *arschina* from them.

There were orchestras of over a hundred pieces, of which the most famous belonged to Prince Kropotkin. Here the second butler was both piano tuner and flautist, the tailor played the French horn, the footman performed on the trombone one day, on the bassoon the next and occasionally took the part of the second violin. The confectioner was first put on the drum, but 'he misused this instrument to such a deafening degree that a tremendous trumpet was bought for him in the hope that his lungs would not have the power to make the same noise as his hands; when, however, this last hope had to be abandoned, he was sent out to be a soldier. Only the first two violins were violins and nothing else', the young Kropotkin writes.

The famous horn music, which was held in high regard, was another example of the low value placed upon human labour. Ker Porter stated that this was invented by a Prince Gallitzin in the year 1767:

'This instrument consists of 40 persons, whose life is spent blowing one note. The sounds produced are precisely similar to those of an immense organ; . . . the effect produces much sublimity, when the *performers are unseen*: but when they are visible, it is impossible to silence reflections which jar with their harmony. To see human nature *reduced to such a use*, calls up thoughts very inimical to admiration of strains so awakened.'

The Russian nobleman may have loved the theatre and the concert, but his behaviour at public performances seems to have left something to be desired. The dramatist, Alexander Sumarokov, felt the need to reprove him in his preface to his work *Dimitri the Imposter*:

'It is unbecoming to sit cracking nuts right next to the musicians and to consider that, once admittance money is paid, it is permissible to engage in fisticuffs right in the stalls, and in the boxes to recount, bellowing aloud, their stories of the past week and to crack nuts. . . .'

A hackney sledge

A family shrove-time outing

So great were the numbers of domestics and so cheaply was human labour valued, that the nobility could afford to indulge its slightest whim. The nobleman, smitten with a sudden desire to erect a pavilion, a triumphal arch or a palace of ice, or to divert the course of a river in a single night, had only to call up the peasants of one or two of his villages, and, with all these assembled and put to work, the job could be finished within a few hours and not a penny to pay for the cost of labour. Whims of this sort were far from unusual in the eighteenth century. Even more trifling idiosyncrasies could be indulged. A certain Countess had in her family several Calmuck women who were taught to read German and Russian. Every night, they read by her bedside until she fell asleep and had to continue reading or talking, without a break, all the time she slept, for if they stopped, the Countess would wake up—none too pleased.

The tables of the nobility showed a similar disregard for expenditure of life and labour in providing nothing but the best for the noble stomach. Martha Wilmot reports on a dinner where 'we had Asparagus, Grapes and everything you can think of and that in weather which is now 26 degrees of cold. . . . The grapes are literally as large as Pigeons' Eggs.' Elsewhere, she describes:

'Dinners that end after *four hours* uninterrupted cramming of every delicacy that Nature and Art can procure—grapes freshly gathered, Pine apples ditto; Asparagus ditto; besides fruit preserved with such care that there is a stout battle between Nature and the Cook for which is genuine, peach, plum etc. etc. etc. I forgot to mention oranges, which are this moment clustering on thousands of orange trees in different parts of Moscow.'

Contemporary memoirs provide a clear picture of the normal pastimes of a nobleman when he was not fulfilling his service obligations. In the morning he went out in his carriage or sledge, according to the season. There was a tremendous vogue for carriages and the 'promenade' was a favourite amusement. All the carriages in the city, sometimes as many as 7,000, would trail after each other in regal procession, through fixed parts of the town and its environs. The Comte de Ségur expresses surprise at this fashion. Everybody above the rank of colonel had to have, according to his position, his own carriage, harnessed to four to six horses, driven by a coachman with a long beard and in full regalia, with two postilions. Each pair of horses had a jockey, a boy of about ten years old who rode the off-side horse and bawled incessantly to remind pedestrians to keep out of the way.

The nobleman dined at half-past two and then either slept for a couple of hours or played cards or billiards. In the evening there were theatrical entertainments or assemblies at his own or his friends' houses, where once again cards were played or a small dance held. Those who preferred to sit it out played on the pianoforte and harp. Various 'little pastimes', such as forfeits and the 'magic music', were brought forward.

Some of these 'little pastimes' were not as sophisticated as the theatrical and orchestral entertainments, and showed the thinness of the veneer of culture covering the Russian nobility. The practice of maintaining fools, dwarfs, hunchbacks and other human curiosities was still continued. Ker Porter compares this custom to the motleys of the Elizabethan English court,

'but like in name only: for their wit, if they ever had any, is swallowed up by indolence. Savoury sauce and rich repasts swell their bodies to the most disgusting size; and lying about in the corners of some splendid saloon, they sleep profoundly, till awakened by the command of their lord to amuse the company. Shaking their enormous bulk, they rise from their trance, and supporting their unwieldy trunks against the wall, drawl out their heavy nonsense, with as much grace as the motions of a sloth in the hands of a reptile fancier. One glance was sufficient for me of these unbruted creatures; and with something like pleasure, I turned from them to the less humiliating view of human nature in the dwarf. . . . Giants are also in request here: but they are not very numerous and in stature fall short of those which occasionally visit England.'

At the same time the Russian nobility particularly enjoyed out-of-door entertainments—cavalcades, promenades and *fête champêtre* in the summer, and sledging parties in the winter. The grounds around their palaces afforded romantic and charming morning walks.

And so to supper. . . . The Reverend William Coxe has his own comments to make on the eating habits of the nobility:

'The tables are served with great profusion and taste. Though the Russians have adopted the delicacies of French cooking, yet they neither affect to despise their native dishes, nor squeamishly reject the solid joints which characterise an English repast. The plainest as well as the choicest viands are collected from the most distant quarters: I have frequently seen at the same table sterlet from the Volga, veal from Archangel, mutton from Astrachan, beef from the Ukraine, and pheasants from Hungary and Bohemia. The common wines are claret, Burgundy and Champagne; and I never tasted English beer and porter in greater perfection and abundance. Before dinner, even in the houses of persons of the first distinction, a small table is spread in a corner of the drawing room covered with plates of caviare, dried and pickled herrings, smoked ham or tongue, bread, butter and cheese, together with bottles of different liqueurs . . . the entertainments are mostly regulated according to the French ceremonial; the wine is circulated during meals and the dishes are no sooner removed than the company retire into another room and are served with coffee. Nor do the gentlemen, as in England, continue wedded to the bottle, while the ladies withdraw into a separate apartment.'

Delicious though these foods may sound, they did not inevitably appeal to an English palate. Martha Wilmot's early comments on a Russian dinner were not altogether favourable.

'Two soups are always brought to table and distributed by a servant, one composed of Herbs, I believe some odious essence of Rosemary or some such thing, ornamented and enriched by lumps of fat—the other is neither more nor less than offer'd *petit pâtees* of bad paste and much worse chop'd Veal, hard Eggs and Herbs. If you don't chose any, you may let it alone and sit looking at those that do till they have done. You are then presented with a Fowl smother'd in butter and boil'd to rags, and the same ceremony goes forward. Next is offer'd vegetables of various kinds and so disguis'd that it requires some Wit to find them out. Next roast Meat, then Wild Boar Ham, and in short such a train of dishes after the same fashion as keeps one hours at table. At length comes the desert, and tho' the fruits are handed about and you must eat according to the servants' taste not your own, yet all their fruit being good this does not signify. The Water Melon is a very fine fruit and grateful in warm Weather as it is Cold as Ice and so juicy that 'tis like a pleasant draught of some agreeable liquid. Coffee follows dinner without removing the cloth or drinking 4 glasses of Wine, Men and Women rising at the same moment from Table.'

It must be emphasised that not all members of the landowning class lived in this state of fabulous affluence. The wealth of a Russian noble was measured by the number of serfs he owned. In 1772, 32 per cent of the nobles owned less than 10 serfs each, 27 per cent between 10 and 20; 25 per cent between 20 and 100. For many of the thousands of serf-owners who owned less than 20 males, life was a constant struggle for survival. They remained on their estates, far removed from the glittering city world, with little chance of ever leaving them. They had neither the time nor the means to care about the amenities befitting their social status. A representative of a group of provincial nobles told the Senate in 1771 that over 200 young nobles amongst the people he represented had informed him that they wanted to enter the imperial service, but did not have the clothes or boots they needed to report for duty. Many adopted peasant ways and peasant manners, tilled their land themselves and sank into the mass of peasantry. One explanation of their sorry plight was the ancient practice of dividing possessions amongst all the heirs, so that at each decease a smaller portion was left to be divided.

Nor was the financial position of many of the greatest lords

A Russian country house

A Russian gentleman

fundamentally healthy. The only way that many of them could live on a scale that they considered worthy of their social position was by borrowing and peculating. They piled up debts proportionate to their eminence; in 1790 Tooke could say that the bankrupt nobles 'live in a sort of affluence and at a greater expense than would be reasonably imagined'. Their heavy indebtedness was partly due to the low salaries paid to government officials and army officers, and partly to the poor return they obtained from their properties. But the improvidence and profligacy of the Russian aristocracy was famous. Thrift could hardly be considered a prime virtue in a period when unspent fortunes might disappear overnight after a palace revolution.

Extremes apart, the personal lives of most of the gentry were rich and even sumptuous. The Reverend Coxe describes the grandeur and magnificence of their houses, domestics and way of living, commending *en passant* their predilection for the English style in arranging their gardens. Their palaces at and near Moscow were stupendous piles of building, and their mansions around Moscow and Petersburg were even grander. Here they lived as independent princes, like the feudal barons in early times, had their separate courts of justice and governed their vassals with almost unlimited sway. Count Orlov's house was typical. It was situated at the extremity of one of the suburbs, upon an elevated spot, and commanded a fine view of the vast city of Moscow and the neighbouring country. It consisted of many separate buildings occupying a large area of land. The offices, stables, riding school and other detached structures were built of brick, as were the foundation and lower storey of the dwelling-house, but the upper part was made of wood, neatly painted green.

Wooden houses were generally thought to be warmer and more wholesome than brick and stone, which explains why several of the Russian nobility chose to build their own apartments in wood. Furthermore, wooden houses were transportable. According to Storch, they could be packed up and moved elsewhere with the greatest ease. In 1787 timber was still the most favoured construction material. Storch estimates that there were 3,431 houses in St Petersburg, of which only 1,291 were built of brick. But as the latter were much larger and loftier, he draws the conclusion that more than half the population of St Petersburg lived in brick buildings—or at least would do if so much room were not sacrificed to ostentation. However, the proportion was rapidly reversing; besides the loss of timber buildings through fire, there was a continual drive to build more houses, and regulations by the magistrature encouraged the use of brick.

Moreover, the brick house had greater style. It normally consisted of two storeys, the lower one used for housing the servants and built of granite. The exterior was generally covered with stucco, painted in gay tints and the roof of iron or copper. Almost all the private houses in St Petersburg had vaulted gateways which protected the family and their visitors from the weather as they got in and out of their inevitable carriages. The family required an immense number of rooms. Apart from the apartments it normally inhabited, a drawing room, a room for receiving visitors, a dining room and an antechamber for the servants of its guests were essential. There were handsome broad stone steps and staircases, balconies to the grand saloons, noble windows with large panes of plate glass, ornamental stoves and chimney-pieces and inlaid floors. Mahogany furniture was in use everywhere, as well as lacquered settees, cushions covered with Russian leather or chintz, large looking-glasses, marble slabs, cut-glass girandoles and lustres, table clocks and carpets. The walls were painted in fresco or hung with paper.

Many of these houses, as we have already seen, were equipped with their own theatres. The oldest and best of these belonged to Count Sheremetev and was built at his Kuskovo estate in the suburbs of Moscow. It was constructed of excellent timber hewn from whole trees to a design by the architect Valli and had a well-built interior, complete with stage, three-tiered boxes and orchestra. The opulence of its theatrical properties can be gauged from the following inventory: eight curtains, 194 settings, 52 side sets, 68 minor decorative accessories, 17 large chests containing brocade, velvet, silk, cloth and woollen wardrobe articles, and 76 chests, boxes and cardboard cases for footwear, costumes and other requisites, such as arms, standards, banners, animal skins, bandores, masks and multi-coloured curtains.

Such was the Russian nobility in its heyday in the latter half of the eighteenth century. During this period, it saw its power increased to an unprecedented extent. A manifesto issued within weeks of the Empress Catherine's accession to the throne proclaimed her intention of:

'energetically protecting the noble proprietors in their lands and properties. . . . Because the well-being of a State, in accordance with the Laws of God and all the laws of the people, requires that all and everyone shall remain upon his estate and shall be assured of his rights, we decide to preserve to the pomeshchiki [landowners] the right to their estates and properties, and to keep the peasants in necessary obedience to them.'

She who had ridden to the throne on the shoulders of the noble Preobrazhensky guard regiment knew all too well the power these forces exercised in making and breaking a Russian monarch. The history of earlier years, filled with palace revolutions, made her need to rely on their support quite obvious—even had her own title to the throne not been so undeniably dubious. Furthermore, she realised that for the enforcement of her laws she must depend on officials who were themselves members of the landowning-gentry class. A glance at the measures

A Russian funeral

she took in this direction make it easy to understand why this was indeed the golden age of the nobility.

A year after her accession to the throne, a commission was set up to revise and confirm the list of privileges her husband had accorded the gentry. Its findings were mostly incorporated in the Charter of the Nobility, issued in 1785, which recognised the nobility as a separate estate with particular rights and privileges. The Charter, amongst other things, once more assured the nobility of its freedom from compulsory service and direct taxation, as well as from corporal punishment and the obligation to billet troops. They were granted permission to dispose of their land and other sources of wealth as they wished; were given the right to establish industrial enterprises on their estates and trade the products thereof both within the country and abroad; to hold fairs and markets on their land; and to possess house property in the towns.

Nobility was to be hereditary and no noble was to be deprived of his rank, except in exceptional circumstances.

As we have already said, the nobles alone possessed the right to own land and serfs—apart that is, from the crown, the state and the church. Their position here became even more privileged by the policy of the monarchs towards the church. Peter III, in his short but so active reign, had found time to place all church property under the administration of an Economic College established for that purpose. Catherine, after some preliminary vacillation, followed his lead. The church peasants were converted into state peasants, 252 monasteries were shut down and 161 others allowed to remain open, only on condition that they were supported by the donations of the faithful. The remainder, together with all other church institutions, were supported by government subventions. The church was thus reduced to the rank of a mere government institution, wholly and officially dependent on secular authorities. The only serious competitor to the power of the nobility had been effectively annihilated.

As far as the ownership of serfs was concerned, the rights of the nobility were similarly supreme. Merchants and manufacturers were forbidden to buy peasants by a decree first passed by Peter III in 1762 —though it must be added that numerous evasions did in practice take place. This prohibition was only lifted in the case of foreigners who came to Russia with Catherine's encouragement to establish factories. Furthermore, the noble's power over his serfs considerably increased during Catherine's reign. It reached a significant climax when, in 1765, he was granted the right to send them to forced labour in Siberia on his own authority and without reference to any tribunal.

This cossetting of the nobility as a class was not limited to the reinforcement of their legal position. Catherine continued the practice of her predecessors in making enormous gifts of land and serfs to the nobles—and on a far greater scale. In the case of her grants of land in the Ukraine (where she introduced serfdom, hitherto unknown there), her generosity can be explained by the economic need to work the rich Ukraine lands where there was no labour. But her other gifts were extremely lavish, and do not appear to have been dictated by any economic criteria. All in all, she is estimated to have turned over some 800,000 peasants, both male and female, to private proprietors. A host of small grants was made: a special event such as a christening in the Czar's family, the cutting of a first tooth by an imperial infant or a military victory were accompanied by awards to the ruler's supporters. Richardson reports: 'The Empress has rewarded Romanzow with the rank of Field Marshal; and has given him a present of 5,000 slaves, corresponding to the number of slain on the field of battle!' Her favourites did even better: Alexander Vasilchikov received 7,000 peasants, 100,000 roubles, a furnished palace worth 100,000 roubles, jewellery worth 50,000, porcelains worth 50,000 and, as if all this were not enough, a pension of 20,000 roubles. More permanent attachments were treated with even greater generosity: Potemkin received a gift of 900,000 roubles on his fortieth birthday, partly in cash and partly in land.

Of course, the nobles did not invariably turn this wealth to economic advantage, by making, for instance, capital improvements to their properties. As we have already seen, many of them took little thought for the morrow and expended prodigious sums on the luxurious living of the present. Here again, the state came to their aid and, to rescue the landlord from the clutches of private money-lenders, took every measure to make credit facilities available to them. The Noble Bank was established in 1754, in 1772 the Foundling Home was ordered to make loans to nobles, and in 1786 the Government Loan Bank was founded with a deposit of 220 million roubles to be lent to the nobles for the improvement of rural economy, of social industry and for the benefit of civilisation in general. The measures applied only to the towns, but the provinces were not neglected. In 1775, the state authorised the charity boards of the provincial governments to make loans to local proprietors and ten years later, by the Charter of the Nobility, provincial credit was still further increased by permission to the noble assemblies of each *guberniia* to form provincial noble banks. In addition to all this, an Assignat bank had been established by the government in 1769 to issue the new paper money and it was also allowed to make loans to important aristocrats by special arrangements.

By the turn of the century, as a result of all these provisions, the government's loans to the landowners actually exceeded its expenditure for all other purposes. But the throne was determined to have an abundance of credit available for its nobility even though this meant cutting back on other governmental functions and straining the state's finances.

The final attainment of the nobility in this period was the realisation of a long-coveted voice in local affairs. Peter the Great had divided his empire into nine extensive governments. After the Pugachev revolt, Catherine began to observe that legislation, whereby each provincial governor was allowed to administer his own province virtually as he wished, was not altogether satisfactory. It led only to evasion of responsibility, difficulty in obtaining reliable information and delay in organising counter-measures. Her local government statute of 1775 broke up the country into units containing an average of only 300,000–400,000 males. These in turn were divided into districts, each with a population of 20,000–30,000. The administrative head of each district was to be elected by the local nobility. Each provincial and district capital was to be provided with separate law courts for the three classes: nobles, merchants, free peasants, with members of each court elected by the class concerned. In each provincial capital, the three elected courts combined to form the public welfare board (mentioned earlier). The nobility of each province and each district elected its own provincial or district marshals.

Thus the nobles gained many more privileges in administration generally, and in the administration of justice in particular, than they had previously possessed. However, the crown was by no means prepared to renounce completely its voice in local affairs. Police supervision in every town remained in the hands of an officer appointed by the central government. The decisions of the elected judges were subject to review by civil and criminal law courts in the provincial capital where all the members were nominated by St Petersburg. The same applied to the officials of the provincial treasury who were responsible for tax collection and other economic decisions. Finally, ultimate responsibility for all provincial affairs rested with the governor and his council—all appointed from the capital.

The Charter of the Nobility extended the powers of the nobility in provincial affairs in that it conferred permanent and official status on the provincial and district assemblies of the nobility and also permitted them to make submissions to the provincial governor and in some cases to the monarch herself.

4   The Serfs

While the small élite of Russian society lived its life in conditions of unprecedented luxury and power, the mass of the population was reduced to a state of moral and physical degradation. 'The peasants in Russia', Richardson writes, 'are in a state of abject slavery; and are reckoned the property of the nobles to whom they belong, as much as their dogs and their homes.'

The great gulf between master and peasant was ever-widening. The master had once been the protector and powerful friend of his peasants. He had become, as we have seen, in a large number of cases an absentee landlord residing in the capital, indifferent to the interests of his serfs and a stranger to their way of life and to the place which had once formed their joint sphere of activity. For him, his village was little more than conquered territory to be exploited as he wished, without consideration for the conservation of its human or natural resources.

While the master lived in a palatial mansion in the city, his peasant lived in the most rudimentary conditions on the land. His house most commonly consisted of one room where the family spent both day and night in company with whatever animals it was lucky enough to own. A few one-storey huts contained two rooms and sometimes, though very rarely, there were even two floors, in which case the lower apartment was a storeroom, and the upper the living quarters; the staircase joining one to the other was most commonly a ladder on the outside of the building. The houses were made of wood, and constructed in a most primitive manner. A number of large trees were stripped of their bark; the wood was not cut into planks but the trunks were laid close together horizontally on top of each other and fastened at the end with wooden pegs to form the walls. The roof was sometimes made of boards, sometimes thatched. Few tools were employed in the construction of these houses; an axe served almost every purpose, even taking the place of a saw. Neither plane nor chisel was generally used—except by professional carpenters. It was amazing what a Russian peasant could do with an axe.

The windows were apertures a few inches square, closed with

87

sliding frames and with dried bladders stretched across them. The doors were so low that even a medium-sized man had to stoop to enter. A large stove or *pech* was the main item of furniture and occupied a quarter of the main room. It had no chimney and belched smoke into the already unsavoury living quarters. However, the warmth it exuded made it the focal point of family life: the flat top served the family for a bed at night; and during the day they lolled around its baking warmth for hours on end. A bed with dirty curtains filled another corner; a few benches and a table hacked out of a tree trunk, two or three pots to hold cabbage soup, wooden cups and spoons and a trough for the pigs and cows completed the furniture. The bare and grimy walls were often brightened by rough prints and innumerable daubings, while a picture or effigy of Christ and the Virgin, sometimes decorated with silver plates, was nearly always hung in a place of honour.

While the master dressed in the latest European fashions, his serfs were clad in skins or coarse woollen cloth and linen, which they used for shirts and under-garments. Over these they wore a large frock, down to the knees, folding over in front and fastened around the waist with a girdle, which was sometimes gay and colourful. Pieces of cloth were

Building a house

Inside a serf's house

A peasant on his travels

wrapped in a variety of folds round their legs, and fastened with strings. They had long beards and wore their hair straight and lank, covering it with worsted or fur caps, usually cone-shaped. A small gold, silver or lead cross hung by a ribbon or string round their necks. They received these crosses from their godfathers at their baptism and kept them religiously throughout their lives. In conjunction with the icons furnishing their homes, these crosses give some idea of the simple faith of the Russian peasant. The women wore sleeveless dresses, with the puffed sleeves of their shifts protruding at the armholes. A scarf covered their heads. On feast days and on occasions when they might be seen by sovereign or nobility, it must be added that the peasants wore the sober, dignified and attractive folk costume of their regions. It is thus that they are usually depicted in the art and letters of the time.

Ker Porter remarks on the strange similarity between everyday peasant garb and that worn by the English in the reign of Richard II. The peasantry of Russia in the eighteenth century were contemporaries in fashion with those of England in the fourteenth.

While the noble feasted at his groaning board, the Russian peasants ate a kind of black bread, made of rye, barley, buckwheat, and other inferior-quality grains; it was sour but not unwholesome, according to Richardson. It was often accompanied by a cucumber, either fresh or

Two peasants

A peasant woman in her summer dress

pickled. The pickled cucumber was prepared by placing alternate layers of oak leaves and cucumber in a cask and covering the whole with salt and water. After a necessary period in a cool cellar it was pronounced ready for use. Cabbage was another favourite vegetable. Large tubs were filled with shredded cabbage; cold water was then poured upon it and it was left until it soured, when the water was drained off. This operation generally took place in August and September when the weather was warm enough to assist fermentation. The casks were put in cellars and the cabbage frozen during the cold winter. It had to be thawed in cold water before being incorporated in a soup. The peasants also ate a great deal of garlic, coarse oil and fish. They made no cheese and were little acquainted with the uses to which milk could be put. Instead, they drank a poor-quality mead, and liquors made of wild fruits; but their chief beverage, of which they made very free use, was kvass, extracted from home-grown cereals.

Whereas the noble was a free man and enjoyed fantastic power over his fellow humans, the peasant was a mere chattel, a possession of his lord, and forming the main constituent and source of the lord's wealth.

Serfdom was no new institution in Russia. Even in the very early days of its expansion the general well-being of the country had clearly depended on the efficient organisation of agriculture. As industry was in its extreme infancy, the principal source of wealth could only be the soil and its products. But the authorities faced the problem common to all countries (not excluding sixteenth-century England) of the shortage of workers on the land. In Russia the difficulties were increased by the very immensity of the country and the character of the peasant, in whom the nomad instinct still survived. He was capable of packing his tent and moving onwards if the land proved unproductive or the surroundings in some way displeasing. The idea of serfdom was based on tying the peasant to one particular estate or one particular master whether the state, the crown, the church or the small or large landowner. In its application, it involved a series of edicts, at first limiting and finally prohibiting the freedom of movement of the labourer.

By the time of Peter the Great, serfdom had progressed to the extent that a considerable section of the peasantry had lost its traditional right of changing masters at will once a year (at a date approximating to Michaelmas). The peasant who ran away was regarded as a criminal. Peter's edicts bound the peasant even more closely to his master, firstly by the poll tax levied on each individual. (The levy of this tax necessitated the introduction of a census— the origin of such statistics as there are for the period.) After 1730, the master was responsible for the collection of the tax and this linked him even more closely with the state against the peasant. There was, in the second place, the passport

A serf dressed in his summer clothes

system, whereby the peasant could not leave his master's estate without written permission—which was only given to the head of the family. Thirdly, the levelling-down process accelerated until all grades of serfs were reduced to a common level of bondage. Furthermore, their numbers increased steadily. Not only did the expansion of the Empire bring more peasants under Russian jurisdiction, but legislation spread the institution of serfdom to this captured territory; and in Russia proper it gave land-owners and factory-owners the power to make serfs out of free men.

The liberation from service that the nobility had acquired in 1762 was not matched by any corresponding concession to the serfs, although the landowners' obligation to serve the Czar had long been regarded as the moral justification for serfdom. When service was no longer compulsory for the nobility, the peasant might well have expected a commensurate relief in his duty to serve his lord. This did not materialise, nor did he gain any advantage from the Free Economic Society or the discussions of the commission. An anonymous serf poet wrote of the commission: 'They are changing the laws to their own advantage; they are not electing slaves as deputies, for what could slaves say there? They would give themselves liberty to torture us to death.'

He was virtually right. The economic and social position of the nobles rested upon the ownership of serfs. Economically, their income came from payments in cash and kind as a result of the labour of these serfs. Socially, their right to own peasants distinguished them from the other ranks of society. It was therefore in their interest to increase the number and win greater control over the lives of the men and women who belonged to them. As the policy of the crown was to retain the support of the nobility at all costs, millions of free peasants were forced to become the serfs of private nobles, who were permitted to reduce these peasants, and the further millions already enserfed, to the condition of human cyphers. Until the eighteenth century, they had at least been restrained by inefficient governmental organisation: some individuals remained outside the social divisions; they avoided paying taxes or services and lived as free men. The modernisation of the central administration under Catherine the Great remedied many of these administrative shortcomings and provided the machinery needed to label everyone as a member of an established social category and introduce many restrictions which prevented his escaping the obligations of his class.

A peasant's house on the edge of a village

The condition of the peasant in every European country was hard at this period. In Russia it was immeasurably harder because of the harsher conditions of work, and because in the eyes of the law the Russian peasant had obligations but no rights.

Let us first consider the question of the peasant's obligations. In 1783, there were some five million peasants in Russia, three million of whom belonged to private landowners, over one million to the church, and the remainder to the crown (apart from a very small proportion of free peasants). The largest section thus belonged to private proprietors and, as each landowner could impose whatever dues and services he wished on his own serfs, the nature and quantity of their obligations varied widely. The lord named a global figure for the village, and the *mir* or village community (a representative body drawn from amongst the peasants) apportioned the land of the village among the peasants

95

and divided the duties among them as it saw fit. The *mir* filled many important functions and, when the village belonged to an absentee landowner, enjoyed a large measure of autonomy under an elected burmister and aldermen. However, the manager of the estate and his clerks were always appointed by the lord.

The *mir* it was that saw in many cases to the redistribution of cultivated land amongst the peasants every few years. This ensured a certain equality in the division of land and prevented the undue enrichment or empoverishment of any individual peasant. But it also provided a factor in the low level of productivity of the soil; there was no incentive to introduce innovations or improvements when ownership was only temporary.

The *mir* served various social functions. When it redistributed the land, it always kept back a reserve lot which was maintained by common labour to provide help for the poor, the aged and anyone who might suffer from fire. The produce from this land was held as a common grain store and supplies were given in cases of need, for example to large families, widows with small children, retired soldiers, old and lonely people and wives of soldiers on service. Often the *mir* employed its collective credit to lease land from the state or private proprietors and even to purchase land—though this transaction had to be conducted in the name of the lord. It sometimes bought supplies in bulk for the village, such as salt, and was even known to own or lease mills.

One of the main services which could bind a peasant to his master was the *barshchina*, the labour obligation. *Barshchina* was fixed annually for farm work on the lord's estate and included winter duties like threshing, or cutting and hauling timber. On some properties, the peasant had to work in the lord's factories or make cloth or other goods in their cottages from material which he supplied. There was no law to limit the amount of labour service that could be demanded and it was not unknown for serfs to do five, six or even seven days' *barshchina* weekly, particularly during the harvest. In these extreme cases, the serfs had to till their own holdings at night or on Sundays and holidays. Radishchev gives a particularly touching instance of this, when he describes an encounter with a peasant working in the hot Sunday sun:

' "You must be a Dissenter since you plough on Sunday."
' "No sir, I make the true sign of the cross", he said, showing me the

three fingers together. "And God is merciful and does not bid us starve to death, so long as we have strength and a family."

' "Have you no time to work during the week, then, and can you not have any rest on Sundays, in the hottest part of the day, at that?"

' "In a week, sir, there are six days, and we go six times a week to work on the master's fields; in the evening, if the weather is good, we haul to the master's house the hay that is left in the woods; and on holidays the women and girls go walking in the woods, looking for mushrooms and berries. . . ."

' "But how do you manage to get food enough, if you have only the holidays free?"

' "Not only the holidays: the nights are ours too. If a fellow isn't lazy, he won't starve to death. . . ." '

The task of making his own land yield a subsistence in the limited time remaining to him was increased by the fact that the peasant tilled the soil with the most rudimentary tools: a wooden plough similar to the one used elsewhere only in the Middle Ages, so light that it could be lifted by hand and drawn by one small horse. The plough-share he possessed was no bigger than a large carving-knife and merely loosened the surface of the earth. Furthermore, he made his own harrows, scythes (also of wood), sleighs, carts and harness.

Other masters went to even more extreme lengths and required their serfs to give up their holdings entirely and work for them full-time. The majority of nobles, however, demanded three days of *barshchina* weekly. A report made in 1780 by a group of St Petersburg landlords stated that the custom was for 'the peasant and his wife to work the year through, half for his master and half for himself'. But in addition to the regular *barshchina*, serf-owners frequently imposed additional days at certain times when more labour was needed, as at hay-making and harvesting.

Obrok—a quit-rent paid in cash and kind—was a far less exacting obligation, and the serfs bound to their lord in this fashion enjoyed a far greater degree of freedom. Originally it was paid in kind, but by the reign of Catherine had mostly been converted into a lump tax or money obligation. Many serfs who paid only *obrok* were able to leave their village and seek work elsewhere.

Apart from the *barshchina* and *obrok*, there were many minor

The Serfs

obligations, such as carting duty, which obliged the peasant to spend days and weeks, usually in winter, transporting goods for his master, frequently produce from the country estate to feed the city residence. For this, he had to use his own horse and cart or sled and maintain himself and his animal during the trip. He could also be called on for building and maintenance work and for service as a watchman.

The whole peasant family was involved in these obligations—not excepting the women, who were kept in a state of continuous industry. When they were not weaving linen or wool—and the noble families required immense quantities of these fabrics, to furnish trousseaux of dozens and dozens of sheets and vast quantities of table-linen—they sewed, helped their husbands in the fields and gathered mushrooms and berries. In *Eugene Onegin*, Pushkin describes the peasant girls picking raspberries, forced to sing in chorus 'so that their naughty mouths do

Transporting produce

not from time to time, eat some of the noble berries'. Furthermore, it was fairly common practice for serfs to be ordered to supply barnyard products at stated times for the lord's table. Special assessments were made if the noble needed to meet expenses incurred by an unusual event such as a visit by the Czar to the region or even an elaborate ball for the gentry in his own home.

These serfs, tied by *barshchina* or *obrok*, at least had their land. The household serfs had nothing. They lived in the lord's palace, serving in the capacity of pastry-cooks, maids, needle-women, nurses, gardeners, carpenters, tailors and so on. Life as a house serf was the most demoralising. In constant contact with the noble family, they were obvious targets for every kind of capricious treatment—and the helplessness of the serfs was a great temptation to the latent sadism of the proprietors. More than any of the others, the house serf was at the mercy of the whims, appetites and tempers of his owner. Martha Wilmot comments, with a certain air of surprise 'Far from considering the situation of Lady's maid advantageous, the Russian peasants usually look upon it as a misfortune to have a child taken to the House of a Noble.' And this despite the fact that 'the servants of the Princess [Dashkov] are in general dress'd much like English sailors, one or two in white linen Jackets and trousers, but of a day that company is expected their liverys are Superb, all embroider'd with lace'.

A nurse

99

The Serfs

The serf-owner took great pride in the unusual skills of his serfs and this eventually led almost to the creation of a new social class: serfs who were not simply domestic servants but craftsmen and artists as well. Apart from the musicians already mentioned, they also numbered many actresses and singers amongst their ranks. Count Sheremetev fell in love with the serf prima donna at his theatre, Praskovya Ivanovna, the daughter of one of his serfs, who used to work in the fields when not on the stage. He married her, but she later died in childbirth. (Her portrait now hangs in the Hermitage Museum.) However, this example is rare and few artistes were as fortunate. They were mainly mere human cattle, subject to the master's caprice, favourites for a moment and liable to be sent back to their village the next. A more typical example is that of the noble lord who suddenly seized the singer playing Dido while in full spate, slapped her face and promised her that, when the play was ended, she would be properly thrashed in the stable. Poor Dido had simply to go on singing. Later, she was indeed banished to a remote village—perhaps because, as a result of venereal disease, she had lost her voice. The story is told by a Frenchman living in Russia.

With orchestras of over a hundred pieces, ballets requiring hundreds of dancers (often nude), teams of decorators, painters and sculptors, a whole world of artistes was created, often taught at great expense by French and Italian masters or even sent abroad to study. Serfs became theologians, engineers, mathematicians, astronomers and architects, but no salary was paid them and they could not move without risking imprisonment. One peasant, who was sent to a German university to study natural philosophy and astronomy, wrote a book on his return which he dedicated to his proprietor.

Apart from the duties they owed their masters, the serfs also had to meet demands from the state. The most formidable of these were the poll tax and military service. Each village was called upon to furnish a requisite number of conscripts for the army. The colonial wars of Catherine and Potemkin and their campaigns against Turkey and Sweden demanded thousands of soldiers annually. As the gentry was exempt from conscription and the merchants could buy themselves off, the full burden fell on the peasantry. Happy was the man who was lame, deaf, blind or maimed; if he did not enjoy such good fortune he frequently cut off a joint of a finger or cut a limb as the time for recruiting approached. At times, of course, army service was a blessed relief from the hardships and capriciousness of life with his master. Radishchev movingly depicts the parting scene as the quota of serfs is removed from the village:

'Here at Gorodnya, some of the recruits have been selected by lot from among the State serfs on the Crown domains in the neighbourhood; others have been handed over by individual landowners, who may send as recruits whichever of their serfs they choose to get rid of. The conscripts take leave of their aged parents or their affianced brides, whom they may never see again, or at least not until their full 25 years' service is over.'

The recruitment system offered numerous opportunities for abuse. Individual wealthier peasants used their own money to buy men they could send into the army in their stead. Even the *mirs* took part in the trade to purchase substitutes from other villages with money levied from their members. Catherine did take measures to limit this commerce in recruit substitutes; in 1776, she decreed that men suitable for military service could not be sold during the recruiting period or for the three months preceding it. But the law was generally evaded. Once again, Radishchev supplies a case in point, telling the tale of three dejected-looking peasants fettered with leg irons and closely guarded. They had formerly belonged to a local squire who needed ready cash in a hurry. Because of the new law, he had to devise other means of disposing of them profitably. He had overcome this difficulty by certifying that he was granting them their liberty voluntarily and had handed them over —for a consideration, let it be added—to the village commune of state peasants who needed some men to complete their quota of conscripts. Thus these three individuals, officially free men, were being dragged off in chains to be enrolled forcibly in the army as 'volunteers'.

Once in the army, however, it was amazing how rapidly the cane could change a clumsy, blundering boor into a neat, active soldier. He was brought from his village with his beard and hair flowing freely, clad in sheepskin, linden shoes and walking with all the trudging awkwardness of unrestrained habit. A very short period changed his aspect entirely. His beard was shaved off, his hair bound in a regular queue and, to make it grow in a more martial form, it was shaven from the forehead over the ears and half-way from the back part of the head. He was enveloped in a regimental greatcoat, booted and set upright: he was now a credit to the Russian Empire.

Apart from the poll tax and conscription the state also called on peasants for lesser dues and services. They could be forced to build and

Flogging a serf

maintain roads and bridges, billet soldiers in their homes or in barracks which they built themselves, supply carts and horses for government use or for persons on official business, furnish postal services and so on. Descriptions of peasants on coaching duty can be found in the memoirs of the time: they were seldom equipped with either boots or saddles; they had no form of stirrup, except a rope doubled and thrown across the horse's back; and they also used an ordinary piece of rope as a whip —though mostly they urged their horses forward with hooting, whistling and catcalls. The wretched harness was continually breaking, the roads were bad and the carriage was often detained for long periods at staging posts while new horses were being procured: travelling was thus a slow process. The conditions under which peasants worked maintaining state roads were equally unsatisfactory. They were often taken from the land and sent indiscriminately and without proper provision to un-inhabited regions far from home where they suffered innumerable hardships, sometimes culminating in death. And in the process the roads received no improvement.

These were the obligations of the peasants belonging to individual landowners. The largest group outside this category consisted of state peasants. They possessed more freedom than the former but still had to pay the soul tax, fulfil, like their fellow serfs, a number of other obligations, and also pay a quit-rent analogous to, but smaller than, the *obrok*. By demanding this rent, the state was asserting its claim to all land not privately owned and confirming its own authority over the peasants living on it. Furthermore, the government could and did give state peasants away as gifts to private proprietors or, even worse, assign them as labourers in industrial enterprises. This hung as a constant menace over the heads of the state peasants.

Another group, the court peasantry, suffered likewise from the danger of being transferred and also from the likelihood of being made to serve as court menials or as the sovereign's peasants. Otherwise, by 1780, the only obligations which remained to the court peasantry were the soul tax, the *obrok*, military duty and the other levies. It was from amongst these groups, as well as from amongst the peasants paying only the *obrok* obligation to their lord, that the first initiative to acquire private wealth, to set up small workshops, to work as tradesmen and to move away from the soil, came.

Finally, there were other groups of peasants assigned to work in industrial enterprises, or used to provide other services required by the state.

The story of the rights of the Russian peasantry, as opposed to that of its obligations, is almost purely negative. During Catherine's reign the state had virtually withdrawn from any supervision and intervention in the relationship between lord and peasant: the serf-owner thus had almost unlimited powers over the people he owned. Furthermore, because of the vast distances in Russia and the difficulties of communications, he did not even need to fear pressure from public opinion —though it is dubious whether he would have met criticism from his peers—and he enjoyed on his estate the prestige of a petty deity. The power that he possessed was rarely entrusted to a private individual anywhere in western Europe—where anyway, after the thirteenth century, the existence of a bourgeoisie mitigated the tyranny of the aristocracy over the peasantry: apart from anything else, the higher urban wages they could offer were an irresistible inducement to flight from tyrannical masters. In Russia, in the eighteenth century, the peasants lived in conditions comparable to those of medieval Europe—but without the buffer of the bourgeoisie.

Of what did the master's power over his serfs consist? He had the right to take anything he wanted from the peasant's property without paying. Custom did not protect the serf if the master decided to increase the amount of goods and services he was required to supply, or to demand that he leave his land and work in the noble's factory, mansion or fields. If this happened he had to obey, for he had no law to appeal to, no court to defend him. In fact, Catherine's reign actually witnessed an increase in the days of *barshchina* the peasant had to work, as well as a rise in the rate of *obrok*.

The lord exercised considerable control over the private lives of his peasants. Marriages were of particular concern to him, as he naturally preferred his serfs to marry one another and so increase the numbers of serfs under his power. A permit from the master was necessary if one serf wished to marry another attached to a different property, and the payment of a fixed sum expected. It was, in fact, a universal custom to obtain the master's permission if the serf wanted to marry at all. The serf-owner often considered that the peasant's obligations included the production of children to add to his assets, and would actually order marriages to take place.

'Marriages of this sort [Richardson comments] must produce little happiness; neither husband nor wife are very studious of conjugal fidelity: hence the lower classes are as profligate as can possibly be conceived; and, in such circumstances, we cannot expect that they will have much care of their children.'

However, not all blame for the low standard of serf marriages can be placed at the gentry's door. A comely peasant wench was not so free from abuse by members of her own social group. It was common practice amongst the peasantry to contract marriages between these hefty young girls and boy babies, so that the household of the latter might acquire the work of an extra pair of hands—and the pater-familias have an alternative companion for his bed.

Radishchev, in his *Description of my Estate* sums up the extent of the master's power over his serfs admirably:

'He can sell him wholesale or retail. This is not said as a joke: for circumstances may be such that the daughter is sold apart from her mother, the son apart from the father, and, it may be, the wife separated from her husband. The master can force him to work as he requires, for the conditions of service of the peasant and the domestic serf are not defined. The master can punish him at his own discretion, he is his judge and executioner of his own verdicts. The master is lord of his property and his children, he bestows and takes away as he likes. He arranges matches and unites in wedlock whomsoever he pleases; consequently the peasant is in this respect a mere bond-slave.'

Radishchev qualifies this statement by conceding that the squire only lacks the right to exempt the serf from government taxation and punishment for criminal offences, or to force him to contract a marriage with a close relative or to eat meat in Lent.

Radishchev was not joking when he said that the slave could be sold. Twice a week, the reading public of Russia was informed by the newspapers that an improvident individual in the landowning classes, had gambled, drunk or given away all his worldly goods, and was adjudged bankrupt. 'At such and such a day, at ten o'clock in the morning, his house will be put up for auction by order of the county court, and with it, the souls of male and female sex belonging to the proprietor. Potential buyers may inspect this desirable property, together with the domestic serfs, on the premises in advance.'

A typical advertisement which appeared in *Moskovskie Vedomosti* (the *Moscow News*) runs as follows:

The Serfs

'For sale—domestics and skilled craftsmen of good behaviour, viz. two tailors, a shoemaker, a watchmaker, a cook, a coachmaker, who may be inspected and their price ascertained in the 4th. district, Section 3, at the proprietor's own house, No. 51. Also for sale are three young racehorses, one colt and two geldings and a pack of hounds, fifty in number, which will be a year old in January and February next.'

It should be mentioned in this context that the price of the serf was often less than that of a pedigree dog and in general the average price varied between 200 and 500 roubles for a man and 50 and 100 for a woman.

Other skills were at a greater premium. An advertisement in the *Moscow News* of 1793 reads:

'A girl of 16 is for sale, a chambermaid possessing a good voice, singing very skilfully, and therefore theatre lovers are hereby given notice that said girl can act cleverly in a theatrical part, and also keep house and cook good meals. The price is to be ascertained at the house of Zobin, near the Church of John the Baptist.'

What price was actually given, we do not know, but some idea of the value attached to skilled serfs can be gathered from the fact that Prince Potemkin paid 40,000 roubles to Field Marshal Razumovskii for a 50-piece serf orchestra.

The logic behind this trade in human beings was quite simple; the land was useless without the worker, therefore the former went with the latter, whether by sale or gift from the crown for services rendered. During the eighteenth century, however, in practice and despite legislation, the movement progressed a step further and serfs could be—and frequently were—sold as individuals not attached to property. Trade in peasants reached its peak during Catherine's reign—even though the Empress made some feeble attempts to remedy the situation. In 1771, she decreed that the spectacle of human beings up for sale should be banned and that the serfs of bankrupt landowners could not be sold at public auctions. Finding these prohibitions disregarded, however, she revised the law to allow sales to take place, but humanely condemned the use of the hammer by the auctioneer.

To be fair, these were not her only efforts to charge the lords with certain responsibilities for the welfare of their serfs. In 1775 she

Religious procession in a village

instructed provincial officials to watch for lords who cruelly mistreated their serfs or who lived so lavishly that they brought ruin on themselves or on their peasants. She also tried to make it more difficult for the lord to free a serf who was too old to work, by ordering that the serf must give his consent to emancipation and that the lord was responsible for the taxes of the freed peasant until the next revision.

However, the restrictions placed on the noble had been basically reduced to two major dogmas: 'the peasant must not suffer ruin' because of the demands of his lord, and he must be allowed enough time to get his own work done. In return, the serf was instructed to give 'silent obedience' to his master in everything that did not contravene the laws of the land.

In practice, the limitation on the lord's power was almost obliterated by the loose phraseology of imperial legislation and unimpeded arrogation by the nobles. Added to this, the investigation of maltreatment or abuse of power was difficult because the serfs were afraid to testify and the accused lord had influence and bribes at his command. Local officials, who were themselves nobles, were obviously strongly influenced in the lord's favour and the government was not very interested because it was so dependent on the nobility.

During the 34 years of Catherine's reign, only six serf-owners are

(overleaf) *Playing on a see-saw*

known to have been punished for cruelty to their peasants. This number probably included the lady at Moscow who was convicted of having put to death over 70 slaves, by scourging and by inflicting on them other barbarous punishments. It was a matter of amusement with her, we are told, to contrive such modes of punishment as were whimsical and unusual. It did not, however, represent by any stretch of the imagination the sum total of cruelty and ill-usage of serf by master. Radishchev's sketch of Mr Assessor may present an extreme example but one that was not so untypical.

'He was avaricious, miserly, cruel by nature, irritable and hence over-bearing with the weak. . . . He made his peasants work on his fields, took away all their land, bought all their cattle at a price which he determined, compelled them to work seven days a week for him and, lest they starve, fed them in the yard of the manor, and only once a day at that. . . . If he thought anyone was lazy, he flogged them with switches, whips, sticks, or cat o'nine tails, according to the degree of laziness.'

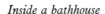
Inside a bathhouse

Elsewhere Radishchev refers to 'the impudence, the crude, unchaste, and offensive jests, with which the audacious gentry assail the village maidens. In the eyes of old and young nobles alike, they are

Inside a tavern

simply creatures for their lordly pleasures. And they treat them accordingly.'

Far from restricting the lord's powers, much of the legislation during Catherine's reign furthered the deterioration in the peasant's economic and legal position. A law of 1763 reiterated the limitations on his freedom of movement by requiring that he obtain a permit from his master before leaving the property. In 1765, the landowners secured authority to send a recalcitrant serf to Siberia without reference to the law and without any right on the serf's part to appeal. In the same year, they were authorised to sentence the serf 'who deserved it' to hard labour with the Admiralty.

(overleaf) *A glissade*

The Serfs

In 1767, the traditional right of the Russian peasant or citizen to present a personal remonstrance (*chelobitnaya*) to the sovereign and to appeal for protection against injustice was suppressed. Violation of this law was punishable by beating with the knout and exile to Siberia. The last legal weapon the serfs possessed for protection against oppression by the lord was thus removed.

The second half of the eighteenth century also saw a series of decrees making it illegal for a serf to contract loans or other liabilities, enter into a lease or work for someone else, without his master's permission. If he obtained his master's permission to borrow, he had to have the master or some other free person as his guarantor.

It can be understood that, given these conditions of life, the character of the Russian peasant was not particularly refined. The European travellers of the period were almost unanimous in blaming his short-comings on his servitude. He detested work because he had never known what it was to work for himself. He could never enjoy the fruits of his labours over and above his needs for subsistence; he could bequeath nothing to his children other than his bondage, what incentive was there therefore to industry—or for that matter, to thrift? He had no interest in anything because he possessed nothing. He had been brutalised by centuries of harsh treatment; treated with inhumanity, how could he be human? It is hardly surprising he sought escape from this intolerable existence in drunkenness.

On the other hand, many of the primary virtues were attributed to him: cheerfulness, kindheartedness, gaiety, honesty and bravery. He was extremely superstitious and hand-in-hand with this went a simple religious faith, witnessed by the icon in his home, the cross around his neck, and the fact that he never neglected to cross himself when coming near a church or even within sound of a bell. He even crossed himself when coming out of doors in the morning, before and after meals, when he received his fare for hiring his sledge, when he began a journey, when he entered any house and also when anything remarkable occurred.

His cleanliness or want of cleanliness was a matter of some dispute. On the whole the verdict was unfavourable though fortunately it was conceded that the peasant retained a few old national customs which from long habit he could not discard and which kept him from total

At the fair

squalor. His table was always scrubbed white, but he had a complete disregard for vermin—or rather treated them with hereditary respect. He washed his body once or even twice or three times a week at the public bathing houses, but he only washed his clothes, however dirty they were, in the bathing room where they were washed at the same time as himself.

Visits to these bathing houses constituted one of the primary pleasures of the Russian peasant. Here he stood or lay on benches round the wall of a steam-filled room. The bathroom had a large vaulted oven, heated so that the stones at the top became red-hot. Water was sprinkled on these stones from time to time; hence the vapour penetrated throughout. The peasant was beaten by the bathing women with dry branches of birch twigs, and then rubbed down with woollen cloths. Now and then he would descend from his bench to the communal tub where buckets of hot and cold water would be poured over him. The baths at St Petersburg had a courtyard with benches where the bathers would dress and undress.

Otherwise his amusements were of the most elementary and appeared almost infantile to the British visitor. He was extremely sociable and liked to assemble with a crowd to sing and drink in the public houses (*kabaks*). A Russian, it was said, never walked by himself, if he could lay hold of a friend; he got drunk in company and rose and fell as one man. He did not tipple for hours but swallowed his fill in a few minutes and lay wherever he fell. But he also enjoyed a swing on see-saws, or a ride up and down and round about in flying chairs fixed upon wheels, some with a perpendicular and some with a horizontal motion. A description of a fair tells of two of these contrivances. One had two cross-beams fixed horizontally to a pole in the centre by a pivot; from the ends of the beams hung four sledges, in which the people sat and were turned round with great velocity. The other had four wooden horses suspended from the beams and the riders were whirled round in a similar fashion. In the winter season, he was pushed down ice hills and glissades, composed of scaffolding of timber covered with ice with steps on one side for the ascent, skated and danced, particularly the famous 'dove dance'.

In the streets in summer, crowds of peasants would kick a large ball stuffed with feathers in a sort of football game, or stand and watch some of their number stage boxing or wrestling matches. They would even be seen playing chess or draughts in the large squares of St Petersburg or under the arcades of the shops.

The Russian peasant was gentle and courteous in his personal contacts with other serfs. Two peasants meeting each other would take off their caps, bow most profoundly, shake hands, wipe their beards, kiss one another and, according to their different ages, call one another brother or father, or by some appellation that expressed affection. If they should happen to quarrel, they seldom proceeded to a duel, as might have been the practice of their western counterparts. They dealt out abuse generously, and their abusive language consisted of the basest allusions and the most shocking obscenity; but at least physical violence was not involved. Many westerners were, on the other hand, charmed by the Russian woman's manner of salutation. She would fold both her hands upon her breast and gracefully incline her head.

5   Industry and Trade

Both consequence and cause of Russia's emergence as a western power was her appearance as a significant economic force in Europe. In 1716, some 320 tons of Russian iron were reported on the London market; by the middle of the eighteenth century she was already an important iron exporter; by the end of the century she was one of the largest iron suppliers of the European market.

The very size of the country and its wealth in mineral resources, coupled with Peter the Great's encouragement to economic advance, explain this development. Though technical progress did not always keep pace with the West, Russia made up in quantity what she lacked in quality. The fact that the mines were so easy to exploit discouraged innovation. Very little change in technique was noted throughout the century, and the machines and processes borrowed from Europe by Peter the Great were still employed at the time of the Empress Catherine's death, nearly a century later.

Nonetheless, her reign marked an important stage in Russia's industrial development: slowly the agricultural Czardom of Moscovy was being transformed into a European industrial nation.

The Industrial Revolution came slowly to Russia. Acting in its favour was a spectacular increase in population from the second quarter of the eighteenth century. This was partly, but not entirely, due to the expansion of Russia's frontiers. Population was estimated at 16 million souls in 1743–45, 19 million in 1762–64, 28 million in 1782–83 and 36 million in 1796. This expanded the potential market for goods and supplied the necessary incentive for speeding up industrialisation.

On the other hand the organisation of the country into large, self-contained estates, where the proprietor purchased little (and that almost entirely foreign manufactures bought from town merchants) and the peasant practically nothing, gave little incentive to the growth of towns. Even in the 1850s a foreign visitor to Russia could write that 'the empire of the Czars, taken as a whole, was just a village'. In 1782, 3·1 per cent of the population lived in towns; in 1796, 4·1 per cent. The

Merchants on the road in winter

comparable figure for England and Wales in 1801 was 32 per cent. It must be borne in mind, however, that much of the Russian population data has a distinct downward bias as it did not always include either peasants who lived in the towns or artisans and traders living in suburbs around the most important cities. Even so, most of the so-called cities were small and many of them were villages in all but name. Catherine's reforms of provincial government in 1775 had to raise some 250 villages to city status to provide centres for her new administrative districts.

Secondly, the size of the Russian Empire made the problem of communications difficult. The roads in the eighteenth century were in an appalling condition and the transport of goods from producer to consumer was in itself a hazardous undertaking. Large quantities never reached the market and the high transport costs involved inflated the prices of those that did. Nor did the government do anything to improve road conditions. River transport offered some alternative to carts on bad roads in summer and sleds on the snow in winter. Here again, however, there were many natural obstacles.

Thirdly, and perhaps most important, was the great shortage of wage labour. Many of the areas where industry was established were sparsely populated; the system of bondage made free labour even more difficult to find. In the West, the Industrial Revolution was carried out by an energetic middle class of merchants through the medium of an urban proletariat. In Russia, neither of these groups existed to any significant degree.

The merchant class in Russia comprised a relatively small number of men, many of whom were commercially inactive. This was partially because an important nucleus of the St Petersburg merchant community were Old Believers. That is to say, in the theoretical sense, they believed in the imminence of God's intervention, specifically to restore the organic religious civilisation of Great Russian Christians united by the traditional forms of ritual worship and communal activity. In practice, it took the form amongst the merchants of an idealisation of the Christian civilisation of old Muscovy, a reaction against Peter's westernisation measures (partly through fear of foreign competition), a resentment of central bureaucracy and a protest against the destruction of the old urban liberties, again by Peter. Their resistance was always passive and took the form of withdrawal into isolated communities of themselves.

But their qualities of abstemiousness and industry were never integrated into building the national culture.

It therefore fell to the state in the reign of Peter the Great to take the first steps towards modern industrialisation. Acting under the need to produce war machines and the desire to increase the prosperity of the country as a whole, Peter established numerous industries including mines, foundries, arsenals, cloth factories and other enterprises to produce goods for his army and navy, and brought in skilled foreigners to direct the plants and train native workmen.

These factories were established by the state to fulfil the needs of the state. But Peter himself also made every attempt to attract men of the merchant class into large-scale factory industry. He offered subsidies, made loans, granted monopolies and even allowed taxation and military service obligations to lapse for the would-be factory owner. He raised import duties on competitive foreign products and removed them from individual imports of machinery required. To a large extent these measures succeeded. Merchants played a major part in the growth of Russian heavy industry. Large fortunes were accumulated almost overnight in a small number of hands. Shcherbatov quotes the example of Tverdchev, a copper manufacturer, who in 1756 possessed nothing but a debt of 500,000 roubles; when he died in 1784, he owned 8,000 peasants, factories and a liquid capital of two and a half million roubles. Again, he cites Tourtchaninov, who did not have a sou when he began, yet became a millionaire within 30 years. And, of course, there was the fabulous Demidov, who was a force of overwhelming importance in the metallurgical industry of the Urals.

By the second half of the eighteenth century, however, many of these fortunes had been broken down by equal division amongst the heirs at the father's death. Furthermore, Catherine's legislation favouring the noble classes at the expense of the merchants tended to encourage a greater number of the landowning élite to interest themselves in industry. A law of 1762 forbade the purchase of peasant villages, with or without land, for factories—though the extent to which this was observed is dubious.

Even without the Empress' encouragement, the nobles already possessed many advantages in the organisation and operation of factories. They had ready supplies of raw materials in the products of their estates.

Distilleries, beet-sugar mills, potash and saltpetre works and other 'agricultural industries' were almost entirely owned by nobles. They also had the labour of their serfs, who worked free of charge as part of their *barshchina* obligation. The lord was free of government restriction or regulation on the way he used his labour—except, that is, for some very general and largely disregarded rules against the mistreatment of serfs. He could regulate his factory production by laying off his serfs without fear of losing them to another employer. He could synchronise manufacturing and agricultural operations and apportion the working time of the serf labourer between factory and field. Finally, transport was also provided by the serf as part of his obligations. It can be seen, therefore, that a noble needed very little capital to start a factory, especially as not much machinery was yet in use.

Many of these conditions had, of course, been in existence for a long time. However, few nobles took advantage of them until the latter part of the eighteenth century. It may have been that the government policies favouring the nobility stimulated interest in industry or that the nobles awoke to the potential of an expanded market. A few nobles may even have realised that industry presented another source of additional income, which could be exploited to meet rising debts.

It is important, however, not to attach too much importance to the increase in the number of factories owned by the nobility. First, many of the nobles registered as factory-owners were in actual fact merchants who had been raised relatively recently to the nobility. Second, many of the lords were merely allowing their peasants to own factories under their names (peasants were, of course, not permitted to own property). In actual fact, only a very small proportion of the nobility was really involved.

The method by which Peter the Great had overcome the shortage of wage labour persisted long after state ownership of factories had become an insignificant factor. The only labour available to the factory-owner in the early years of industrialisation consisted of criminals, fugitives or bought serfs. Peter met this difficulty by compelling peasants to work at the factories as forced labour. This was first done by an individual *ukaz* relating to a specific factory, and granting to it entire villages of state peasants to pay by their work for the total of their taxes. These peasants were only to provide additional labour. The theory was that the peasant should work for a short period during the winter months for the factory-owner and be free during the crucial summer periods to return to cultivate his own portion of the soil. The peasant, again in theory, belonged to the factory and not to the factory-owner.

As the practice developed and state encouragement to industry continued, grants of peasant villages no longer required an individual *ukaz* but were automatically made to whomsoever decided to construct a factory of a specific size. Anyone starting an iron mill could get 100–150 families of peasants assigned to his plant for each blast furnace he operated and 30 households for each forge. Copper smelters could get 50 households or 200 male peasants for every 1,000 *pudy* of refined copper they produced.

The duties required of these peasants gradually increased, and at the same time they came to be regarded more and more as a chattel belonging to the master and not as attached to the factory. In fact, they could find themselves moved to another factory under the same ownership far distant from the village.

It was equally an easy process for this 'additional' labour to extend until it occupied almost the entire year. The rhythm of work was determined by the seasons. Winter was the time for transporting along the snow-covered roads, which quickly filled with long caravans. Minerals, charcoal and even cast-iron, *en route* for the processing works, were moved along the poor roads of the Urals and very rarely travelled by water. The peasant assigned to transport worked with his own sturdy little horse which in summer browsed peaceably on the clearings. The rivers on which the factories were built were only useful for transport at the time of the spring floods: caravans of barges laden with iron bars and finished products would then set sail on 1 April. The additional labour employed in the spring had to be particularly heavy, because, while one team was engaged in loading barges, another was needed for cutting timber. The minerals and stone were generally extracted in summer and autumn. Here again, work overlapped and required large numbers of workmen.

The gap between the free labour—the criminals, fugitives, etc.—that the factory-owner employed and the assigned serfs diminished as the century progressed and state legislation tied the free labourer to the factory. By the second half of the century, virtually the same conditions applied to both types.

Industry and Trade

By the reign of Catherine, life was appallingly hard for these peasants. Apart from their hatred of compulsory labour at distasteful work in unhealthy conditions, for low, or uncertain remuneration, they were temperamentally unsuited to the type of work involved. They were accustomed to the slow and leisured pursuit of agriculture, passionately devoted to the soil and unaccustomed to large-scale mechanical employment or underground working conditions.

Furthermore, they resented large-scale industry which seemed to conflict with the tradition of homespun, better-quality goods and—more important—which was in competition with the peasant products on the market. A tradition of discontent grew up amongst the ascribed workers of the Urals, expressed in their popular songs and transmitted from generation to generation:

> *Work is hard*
> *at Demidov's factory*
> *Oh but the work is hard,*
> *And how our backs ache.*
> *They put a bath in our factory*
> *But they never let us leave.*
> *Oh forests, forests of high timber*
> *Thick forests of the mountains*
> *You hide fine fellows, fugitives*
> *The poor devils who have become brigands*
> *Alas for the workers of Demidov!*

The peasants of Nevyansk in the Urals complained:

'we cut wood for charcoal and drive it to the blast furnaces. We drive timber to the works; we drive iron and other military supplies to the River Chusoraya where we build rafts and float them to Moscow. And we do this without pay, though for the voyage we have to send about twenty men whom we have to hire at a very expensive rate. And the manager holds us at the works for driving and cutting timber four weeks and more and we suffer from him great misfortunes and hunger because the cutting of timber is done in the winter when the snow covers everything.'

The original idea that the peasant should only work four months of the year at the factory and have the remaining eight months to work for himself on his own land in the village, had, as we have seen, not withstood the test of time. In practice, the peasant had many other chores to perform at the factory and in some cases, would remain there for eleven months of the year, with only four weeks for his own work.

This could frequently cause much suffering to his family who remained at home. The villages were left in a state of gloom and

Making guns

deprivation. A traveller of the time, Lepekhin, reports on badly built houses, depressed and impoverished inhabitants. At Selitsche, he found one crippled old man, all the rest of the people were at obligatory labour at the works of Pokhodyashin. 'Poverty has brought them to such a pass, that in the villages the women and children are, during a great part of their lives, obliged to satisfy themselves with the bark of the fir, which they grind down, and mixing it with a little rye flour, bake cakes of it.' Peasants at the works of Nikita Demidov report:

'We were sent away from our houses to the heaviest labours at the works, and in our homes there were left only our wives and children, with the old and invalid people who cannot work, who could not only not plough and seed in spring and autumn, but could not gather the seeded crop from the fields and these, on account of neglect and other causes, were damaged by beasts.'

Furthermore, the factory was often at some distance from the village and, as we have also seen, in some cases proprietors would transfer workers ascribed to one factory to another in their possession. This

A factory worker

could result in a journey from works to village, lasting some four to five weeks—a journey which could hold great dangers. Stories are told of peasants freezing to death or becoming totally lost on the way. It was also somewhat costly, requiring horses or other means of transport. Where distances were excessive, the peasant had frequently to sever his connection with the land.

The factory peasant often lived huddled in groups of 200–300 in barracks belonging to the factory-owner. The factories were run with military discipline and this was matched, in the case of the metallurgical factories of the Urals, by the defensive appearance of the building itself. It consisted in many cases of a fortified enclosure made of a stockade with watch-towers. The type had originated in the early days of development when the factory had to be defended against Bashkir attacks—and also from the need to hold in check a working force of unwilling slaves. It was perpetuated even when the actual need had passed. Furthermore, the factories often served as defence centres for the surrounding area and were frequently better defended than the military posts. It was common custom for them to supply detachments to escort convoys of metal to the embarkation point or to answer calls to put down revolts in other factories or villages.

Living conditions here were anything but sanitary. No more so were the conditions in which the peasants worked. It was said that in the cloth factories, which had sprung up through the need to produce uniforms for the army, the majority of buildings where weaving was carried on were so badly lit that the worker could barely see what he was weaving. Details of the length of the working day are only available for state enterprises, but these are formidable. The prescribed length of work varied between $12\frac{1}{2}$ and $13\frac{1}{2}$ hours a day between 10 March and 10 September. For the remainder of the year, the day began one hour before sunrise and ended one hour after sunset, with an hour for rest allowed during the day. On Saturdays, work was supposed to cease three hours before evening. This, however, was purely theoretical and there are many reports of peasants having to work on Sundays and holidays, without payment.

Wages were in any case grossly inadequate. Old people and children often had to go out and beg, in order to earn the minimum needed for bare subsistence, even though all their active men- and womenfolk were gainfully employed in the factories. The ascribed peasants at the Yugovsky works complained that piece-work wages were insufficient, for 'food, clothing and shoes'. They could not pay their taxes because they had been deprived of their last property and their last food and had no houses.

Punishments inflicted were also severe, ranging from fines to fetters to all forms of corporal punishment with sticks, rods and knouts. There were many stories of ill-treatment, varying from peasants being beaten, because they refused to work in the factory at harvest time, to workers being thrown into blast furnaces or confined in the underground chambers of the factories and drowned. It was not safe, moreover, for the peasant to complain because not only were the mountain works far from government centres but the owners exercised magisterial powers. As a result, petitioners were frequently dismissed with a flogging. Often workers would, from their tiny wages, pay bribes to their superiors to escape punishment.

Peasant unrest was so great and petitions so frequent that a commission was formed in 1762 to investigate all cases of dissatisfaction. Catherine appointed as its president one Prince Vyazemsky whose main title to the office was that he had shown great strength of character in pacifying the peasants on his own estate. He had ordered 20 peasants to be shot. He was instructed that the peasants should be compelled to work and therefore must 'be brought into the usual slavish obedience'. When he was recalled slightly over a year later, he had 'pacified' ten works, punished 235 people, 38 with the knout, 88 thrice with lashes, 83 once and 26 were beaten with rods.

Not until the period 1779–81 did the state make some attempt to ameliorate the workers' lot. It ordered improvements to be made in working conditions, placed limitations on the factory-owners' powers to punish and ordered an increase in wages to double their pre-1769 level. However, an additional two roubles on the capitation tax partially absorbed this increase. A decree stated that peasants assigned to the mines, the property both of the crown and of private proprietors, should as before provide for the necessary labours at the mines. That is to say, they should be responsible for the felling of timber for burning into charcoal; for breaking up the coal-heaps and carrying the coals to the works; for chopping wood for the fusion of the metals; for conveying the ore obtained to the works and also the necessary sands and fusions; and for making and repairing dams, but only in cases when they had been damaged in inundations or fire. The peasants were not bound to perform any other work whatsoever, but neither were they forbidden to undertake it voluntarily by agreement. They should be taken on at the beginning of the winter and should be discharged at the melting of the snow, so that they might attend to their agriculture. A labourer with a horse should receive ten kopeks daily in summer and eight in winter. At these wages they should work out their head money, amounting to 170 kopeks; but should not be required or obliged to perform any further labour.

But serf labour—like any forced labour—was on the whole un-satisfactory. In the ironworks, the serfs laboured slowly and unwillingly, conscious that the metal they were helping to produce would be used to make cannons to mow them down if they dared revolt. In the silk factories, they acquired a downright repugnance for silk culture and sprinkled the worms with salt water to kill them. Factory-owners gradually came to realise that the productivity of forced labour was low in relation to hired and willing workers. Towards the end of the eighteenth century, therefore, a new trend is evident. At the outset, hired labour had consisted solely of city dwellers, runaway serfs and people not attached to any class. But as the demand for hired labour increased, the factory-owner looked to the peasantry, and simultaneously more and more serfs were able to obtain permission to leave their villages and convert their *barshchina* obligation into the payment of *obrok*.

In the latter half of the century, the factories and workshops were becoming technical schools, turning peasants into skilled mechanics. The state factory at Ekaterinburg was something of a model in this respect and its school for apprentices was famous. The factories in the early days had profited from the instruction of foreign workmen, but these rarely stayed for long periods and therefore the need was felt to replace them by native skilled craftsmen. By the end of the century, there was, as we have just seen, an increasing number of Russian free labourers working for wages, recruited partly from residents in towns, but mostly consisting of peasants released from personal bondage by paying *obrok*. However, this development was slow and in 1794 there were still reckoned to be some 80,000 possessional peasants.

A parallel trend was the increase of peasants who were factory-owners themselves—often while still serfs, holding their factory nominally in

A tradesman

their master's name as, of course, no serf was legally permitted to own property. It was, in a sense, in the lord's interest to encourage this initiative as affluent peasants were better able to pay higher *obrok* rates. It is interesting to note that the noble landowners were much more willing to support peasant initiative than merchant enterprise. It seemed to them vastly preferable to encourage the development of widespread peasant industry in the hands of small craftsmen than industry concentrated in the hands of a small number of bourgeoisie, who might through their increasing wealth and importance acquire political power.

The peasant factory-owner began his manufacturing career as an artisan working in his own house or in a workshop. Gradually he began to farm out work amongst his fellow peasants and eventually opened a small factory (which in some cases grew to considerable size). The village of Ivanovo, which became the cotton textile centre of Russia, acquired an exceptional number of peasant-owned factories. At the end of the century, a peasant called Sokov returned to Ivanovo from a job in a plant that printed cotton cloth and opened his own factory. Other peasants learned the trade from him and soon cotton-printing was the main occupation of the village. Although plants belonging to peasants formed only a small proportion of Russia's large-scale manufacturing establishments, the importance of the peasants outweighs the merchant class and the nobility. This is very largely due to the key position of the local handicraft industry (*kustar*) carried on by peasants in their homes. The success of this industry meant that the peasants employed in it were comparatively well off. They lived in better-built houses, wore leather boots instead of bast shoes and were able to buy things they required rather than make everything they needed themselves.

The number of factories in Russia, however, increased during Catherine's reign. Somewhat dubious figures give some indication of the growth: in 1762, when she ascended the throne, there were 984 factories in Russia, excluding the mountain ironworks; when she died the quoted figure was 3,161. This expansion resulted, as we have seen, from a combination of circumstances: from the relaxation of state control over industry; the increase in urban population (which was both cause and effect of growth); from the greater number of peasants paying *obrok*; from the increased loans and credit facilities the Empress had made available.

But when we look more closely at the factories that existed in Russia at the end of Catherine's reign, the fact emerges that they were mainly for processing raw materials. It had proved much more difficult to stimulate production of consumer goods such as silk, paper or glass on any significant scale. Of the 300 most important industrial enterprises of this type in the country in 1780 only 22 had survived from the reign of Peter the Great. Foreign competition, shortage of skilled labour and the lack of an internal market in a peasant country (which mostly supplied its needs from abroad or from peasant handicraft industries) were all contributory factors in this high rate of turnover.

Porcelain, however, was a notable exception. Peter the Great had

A vase from the Imperial Porcelain Factory

A broomseller

already dreamt dreams of manufacturing porcelain in Russia and had sent scientific experts to Peking to discover the 'secret' method involved. They had returned disappointed. The Imperial Porcelain Factory only came into its own during Catherine's reign. In 1763 the Empress made a thorough personal inspection of the factory and ordered highly skilled painters, modellers and craftsmen to be engaged from Germany, Austria and France. Many private factories also prospered, including an important one started in 1756 by an Englishman, Francis Gardner, in the Gjelsk region where the white clay was well suited to porcelain. Gardner first employed a German manager and painter, but they gradually instructed the serfs, and the number of foreigners in key positions diminished.

But porcelain was one of the relatively few exceptions, and at the end of the century Russia was still an exporter of raw materials and semi-finished products—timber, hemp and, of course, iron primarily—and an importer of manufactured goods.

Trade during Catherine's reign soared. Imports rose from 8·2 million roubles in 1762 to 39·1 million roubles in 1812–15, and exports from 12·8 million roubles to an annual average of 62 million roubles. Here again, the improvement can in part be attributed to government action. The issue by Catherine of large quantities of paper currency in 1769, the abolition of internal tariffs, the ending of monopolistic privileges and the establishment of freedom of enterprise by the removal of the barriers which prevented any free man from entering any branch of trade or industry—all these played their part.

But even an un-free man was occasionally able to cut in. There was,

A merchant talking to a peasant

The wife of a Russian merchant in her gala dress

as we have already said, only a small number of men in the merchant class, unevenly distributed over the Empire, and many of these only nominally traders. A government study in 1764 estimated that only 1·9 per cent of the urban population (excluding nobles, clergy, bureaucrats and peasants) was engaged in inter-regional or foreign trade, and 40·7 per cent traded only within the limits of their home town. The remainder were artisans, labourers or unemployed. Persons who registered as merchants often earned their livings in other fields. Some towns had no merchants at all. This presented another opportunity for the enter-prising peasant. In doing so, he was breaking a law which restricted trading to men registered as members of the merchant class, and another which forbade him to own any form of business in towns and only allowed him to carry on trade at town markets and then only from wagons or barges. But he could disregard these laws with the connivance of his lord, who in many cases, was prepared to protect him, realising that there was a need for this service and also that, once again, a prosperous peasantry could be to his own advantage in enabling him to raise the *obrok*.

The process of development was much the same as in the case of the peasant factory-owner. At the outset, the serf mainly entered trade in order to supplement his scanty earnings from agriculture. Some became part-time pedlars or small merchants; the more enterprising bought up the output of their fellow villagers for resale. Others moved into the cities and opened shops—but always under the name of their lord. Thus whole rows of shops in St Petersburg bore the name of Sheremetev.

The small merchant class also contained a number of foreigners. The expansion of trade ensured that it lived in fairly prosperous conditions. But these merchants, despite their wealth, did not generally follow the trends of the nobility towards westernisation and education, though, in the physical trappings of affluence, they were their equals, if not their betters. There was, for example, Pokhodyashin, who had begun his working life as a carpenter and carrier and then became a merchant and had had mountain works granted him by the crown. His mode of life is typical of many of his class. His wooden house at Verkhoturye (to own a stone house was a symbol of affluence) had 30 luxuriously decorated and furnished rooms wherein he was accustomed to entertain high dignitaries of the state. Yet he was exceptional in being regarded as a good man, who built and decorated churches, gave charity on Saturdays and was kind to his peasants (there were 4,200 of them at Petropavlovsk alone). Nonetheless, he is stated to have kept them in a state of absolute dependence.

The merchants' wives paraded the physical trappings of their wealth.

'They were dressed in all the riches their husbands could afford, in a fashion hot, stiff and most discordant with their figures . . . every point about these dames is the opposite of beauty. Their eyes are tolerable, but totally divested of expression. Their complexions are besmeared with white and red paint and their teeth most perversely stained with black; not a muscle of their face ever moves: and in general, their usual attitude being stationary (hardly ever walking) with their hands knit together across their persons, they stand like a string of waxen figures, gazing at the passing groups of the higher orders.'

Martha Wilmot confirms this:

'In one of the warmest days that ever came, she [a merchant's wife] was arrayed in a jacket and petticoat of Damask brocaded richly with gold, stomacher distinct and chiefly composed of pearls, a plated border of pearls as if it was of muslin formed the front of her cap, while a building scarcely half a yard high composed of pearls and diamonds completed the headdress. On her neck were twenty rows of pearls, and on her massy arms hung twelve rows by the way of bracelets. Thus arrayed, she walked by the side of her bearded husband, whose dress was likewise the native dress of the country, a coat of green velvet, with a sort of petticoat skirt reaching to his heels and embroidered all round with gold, flat crown'd hat etc.'

Their fur hats in winter might be either helmet-shaped or low with a brim. The traditional Russian high boots were gradually being replaced by low shoes, worn with stockings. And of course, the beard persisted.

Their city houses were not palaces, but were, nonetheless, extremely comfortable and mainly boasted gardens. They had their dwellings and computing houses in the most elegant parts of the city. Their houses, gateways and courtyards were not, as in Hamburg and Riga, blocked up and barricaded with bales of goods and heaps of timber. They ate well although de Ségur comments that the Russian merchants, when they had become rich, displayed a tasteless and boundless luxury on their tables.

'They serve one with fearful piles of meat, poultry, fish, eggs and pastry piled higgledy piggledy, offered to the guests with importunity and capable by their very quantity of frightening off the most intrepid stomach.'

6 Revolt

Circumstances of such blatant social inequality made revolt inevitable. It appeared almost simultaneously in the dual form of serious physical violence from the peasant classes and of intellectual protest by a growing group of alienated intelligentsia drawn from the nobility.

Relatively minor outbursts were a commonplace occurrence amongst the peasants and factory-workers. Given their state of oppression, no degree of lasting contentment could be possible and their dissatisfaction erupted from time to time in the form of passive protest, such as the refusal to work or to pay *obrok*, or more actively in actual rebellion when they burned the master's house to the ground, raided his granaries, broke factory machinery or even attacked and murdered the master and his family. However, these small-scale sporadic disturbances could, on the whole, be quelled without undue difficulty by the noble himself, or, if necessary, by state military intervention. In fact, in 1763, the Military Collegium or War Office found it advisable to issue general regulations for the conduct of military operations connected with peasant disturbances.

But in 1773 something of a more serious nature shook the Russian state to its foundations. The peasant classes found a leader able to unite them in their grievances and cause a disturbance of such serious significance that it even moved the Empress to anxiety in her sheltered haven at St Petersburg. The man capable of seizing the psychological moment when hope was at a maximum and want was not so great as to emasculate hope, was Emilian Pugachev, a Cossack from the Don area. In his youth, Pugachev had been an irregular horseman in the regular army and as such had fought in Catherine's campaigns in Poland and Turkey. On his return, he had had more than one clash with the authorities and been sentenced more than once to imprisonment. From a final jail sentence, Pugachev escaped and reappeared to inaugurate one of the bloodiest periods in Russian history.

His policy was cleverly conceived. He succeeded in playing on practically every grievance cherished by the superstitious and gullible

Pugachev, the impostor

peasantry. Claiming to be Peter III (the murdered husband of the Empress), who had escaped his assassin's clutches and returned to save his people, he exploited a long-held belief that Peter, when he promulgated his edict of 1761 freeing the gentry from their service obligations, had intended to follow it by another freeing the peasants from their obligations to serve their masters. He went to great lengths in his capacity as would-be Czar, providing himself with Czarina, court and heir and living in sumptuous splendour. Most of his followers had never seen the Czar, but they found the call to follow the 'Little Father of all the Russias' irresistible. They were happy to accept this stout fellow with black beard, gold-embroidered caftan and fur cap covered with medallions, surrounded by splendid black-bearded officers, as their sovereign returned to redeem them from slavery at the hands of the foreign usurper on the throne.

Pugachev also appealed to religious discontent. An Old Believer himself, he announced that 'we shall make the true faith prevail and take over the land for ourselves'. He found ready support for this ambition amongst the Cossacks who were mostly Old Believers, had suffered from the church reforms and were convinced that these reforms, which seemed merely to advance the interests of the upper classes while continually worsening their own, were the main cause of their wretched condition. Furthermore, the country had recently been ravaged by a cholera epidemic which opportunely seemed to indicate that the wrath of an outraged deity had been aroused. Pugachev, therefore, found little difficulty in rallying support under a religious banner and the Cossacks were amongst the first to join him.

The recent wars with Poland and Turkey, with their great expenditure of life—mainly peasant life at that—provided further grounds for discontent. But finally and most significant, Pugachev played on the great sense of social injustice from which the workers suffered. In 1774, at Chelyabinsk in the Urals, the following manifesto was issued:

'Our Lord Jesus Christ deigns to desire, through Holy Providence, to free Russia from the yoke of servile toil, a toil, I tell you, which is known the world over. . . . You yourselves know how Russia is being used up and by whom: the nobility own the peasants, and although it is written in the law that they are to treat them like their children, yet they look on them merely as slaves, and lower than their dogs they keep for hunting hares. . . . Factory owners have set up a mass of factories and they work their serfs so that nothing like it is seen even in the prisons. How many are the tears shed by the workers and their wives and their little children! But, like the Israelites, you shall be delivered out of bondage.'

His programme gave more concrete expression to the manner in which he proposed to tackle the social problem.

'You, such as you are, I enfranchise you and give eternal freedom to your children and grandchildren. . . . You will no longer work for a lord and you will no longer pay taxes: if we find you toiling on behalf of another, we will massacre you all . . . we grant all those who have hitherto been peasants and the serfs of landowners the privilege of being the most faithful slaves of our own crown; we make them a gift of the cross and of their ancient prayers, of the long hair and the beard, of liberty and independence. . . . When we have destroyed their enemies, the guilty nobles, each man will be able to enjoy a life of peace and tranquillity which shall endure for hundreds of years.'

He furthermore declared that the landowners were pernicious to society, ruinous to the peasantry and traitors to the Empire. The serfs were exhorted to treat their masters as the latter, who were persons devoid of all Christian feeling, treated them. Following the extermination of the

A Cossack

squirearchy, Pugachev promised there would be no more recruiting levies or taxes; the peasants would own the land, have unrestricted access to meadow lands, fishing rights and the use of wood and timber, and general deliverance from 'imposts and burdens previously imposed on peasants and the entire nation by the villainous gentry and the corrupt city judges'. It is interesting to note that these diatribes are supposed to have been composed by an illiterate Cossack from the Don—even though some sources grant him a secretary. It would appear possible or even likely that some more literate pen from a more literate class may have given assistance.

Pugachev found his first followers amongst the Cossacks of the Urals, a community in a continual state of greater or lesser conflict with authority. They were wilder than the Don or Volga Cossacks, closer to their ancestors, the rough Mongolian horsemen of the steppes, and they were tired most particularly of existing as a small minority group in a foreign land, oppressed by leaders in the pay of the government. They had aspirations to carve a kingdom of their own out of the Urals and this was shared by other indigenous populations along the shores of the Caspian and the lower Volga: Kirghiz and Bashkirs, Moslem Mongols recently subdued by the Russians and all the more resentful as an attempt had been made forcibly to convert them to Christianity.

These were Pugachev's first allies. But revolt spread rapidly and could not fail to attract the peasants and workers whose grievances needed but small encouragement to take active form. What is more, Pugachev actually sent out his men to gather active supporters; they found few who were not willing to rise to obtain their emancipation from the nobles. And Pugachev's men, skilled, if not professional soldiers, were able and prepared to train their host of new recruits into a very presentable army. By the end of November 1773, he had gathered together a considerable troop, invested Orenburg and shortly afterwards was able to withstand the imperial force under Karr sent from St Petersburg.

The revolt continued, Karr was replaced by Bibikov. But still Pugachev gained support. Workers and peasants flocked to his ranks as they moved northwards through the provinces of Ufa and Perm and finally neared the city of Kazan. He received support from other unexpected sources: many of the regular troops had grounds for complaint and were happy to join forces with—or at least not to offer over-strong resistance to—the insurgents; the clergy, too, alienated by

Pugachev in chains

Catherine's policy towards the church, tended to side with them. Finally the rebels had the great advantage of familiarity with the terrain, not shared by the St Petersburg forces.

Pillaging, sacking and burning every noble estate *en route*, murdering every nobleman they encountered, raping every noblewoman—so that Moscow was besieged by panic-stricken noble refugees—the troop approached Kazan. On 12 July 1774, the town was stormed and burned to the ground. But the end was in sight. At the rebel encampment outside Kazan, Pugachev met his first defeat. He regathered his forces to fight again, but to no great avail. Pugachev was captured and brought to Moscow in a cage to await execution.

At the same time as Russia was being profoundly shaken by this uprising amongst the masses, the first rumblings of a new critical movement at the other end of the social scale could be detected. The beginnings of a social conscience amongst the nobility was marked by the formation of a new Russian intelligentsia.

It is not surprising that this first generation of the Russian intelligentsia should have been drawn from the nobility. They were the only active élite in the country in the second half of the eighteenth century; their outlook had been continuously broadened since the reign of Peter the Great; they had been given by the introduction of compulsory education the basic cultural weapons to enable them to think for themselves; they had come into contact with life and ideas abroad by their newly gained liberty to travel and also by the encouragement given to foreigners to visit Russia. All these had had a profound influence on their own attitudes.

Some members of this intelligentsia inevitably turned their attention to the state of their own country, and, when they did, found it sadly wanting. Three great names stand out in this first display of intellectual independence: Radishchev,

Radishchev

Radishchev on the road from St Petersburg to Moscow

Novikov and Fonvizin. The criticism which emerged roughly followed
two lines: social criticism directed against the economic inequality and
injustice in eighteenth-century Russia; and a cultural approach which
blamed this state of affairs on the Europeanisation of the country
and went from there to seek a national Russian culture of its own.

Radishchev was the leading representative of the social critics. He
was the first important example of the large group of conscience-stricken
gentry obsessed with the idea that it, as a class, was enjoying illicit
privileges at the expense of the peasant masses. He was anxious to make
reparations. He was in no sense a revolutionary. He merely depicted
the situation as he saw it and pointed to the revolution that was inevitable,
if it were not reformed.

Alexander Nikolaevich Radishchev was born in Moscow in August
1749 into an educated family of landed gentry. Until he was eight
years old, he lived on his father's estate at Verkhovnee Oblyazovo. He
then spent the years from 1757 to 1762 with his mother's family in
Moscow and from 1762 to 1766 was a member of Catherine's exclusive

Corps des Pages in St Petersburg. This body consisted of some 60–70 young nobles who, while they performed the usual services at the court, were also trained to fill civil or military callings. They left with the rank of lieutenant or captain. He was then sent by the government to study at the University of Leipzig. He returned to Russia in 1771, entered the civil service as a clerk of the Senate and remained there until 1790, apart from a short break in the military service. By then he had risen to the lofty rank of Chief of the St Petersburg Custom House. In that year his most important work, *A Journey from St Petersburg to Moscow*, appeared and his career came to an abrupt end.

The book takes the form of a series of short sketches of scenes and encounters with people and is filled with thinly veiled, or at times, outspoken social criticism. Radishchev saw all too clearly the evils of serfdom and pointed them out in logical sequence. In the first place, it was wrong in that it was a violation of natural right. He was, in this, the first Russian writer to invoke the ultimate moral law, the rights of man: all men are born free; to enslave one's fellow men is wrong. Wrong, too, that the man who possesses the natural title to the land should be totally excluded from all rights of ownership and should depend for his means of subsistence on the whims of another.

In the second place, serfdom was economically undesirable as it deprived the peasant of the incentive to work hard. In Russia, where the land and its product belonged to someone else, the peasant worked languidly and without enthusiasm. 'The spirit of property doubles a man's strength', he says, and elsewhere in the *Journey*, a peasant he meets in Lyubani describes the tremendous efforts he makes to accomplish the work in his own fields. Radishchev asks him, 'Do you work the same way for your master?' 'No, sir, it would be a sin to work the same way. On his fields there are a hundred hands for one mouth, while I have two for seven mouths. . . . No matter how hard you work for the master, no one will thank you for it.' The low productivity of the land tilled by the serf directly obstructed the growth of population and was one of the main causes of the dreadful famines which from time to time brought starvation to the Russian countryside.

Finally, serfdom was morally wrong, corrupting both the master and the serf. It resulted on the one hand in arrogance, on the other in servile fear.

145

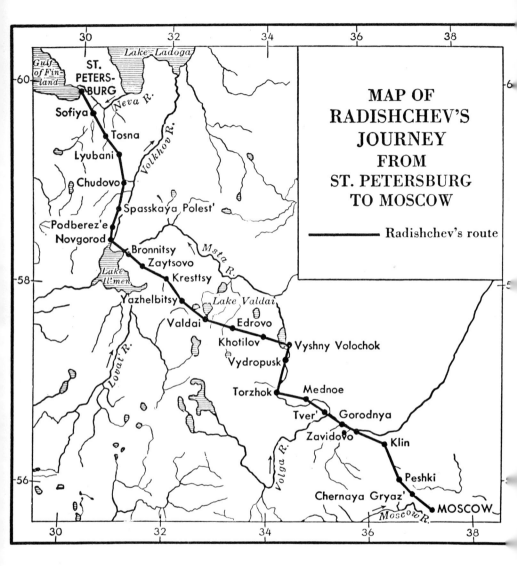

MAP OF
RADISHCHEV'S
JOURNEY
FROM
ST. PETERSBURG
TO MOSCOW

——————— Radishchev's route

What was Radishchev's remedy for this situation? Not, as we have already said, revolution. He had concrete proposals to put forward. The first related to the separation of agricultural serfdom from domestic slavery. The latter should be abolished, and it should be forbidden to turn peasants, or anyone included in the village census returns, into

146

domestic bond-servants. If a landowner took a peasant into his mansion for domestic service or other work, then that peasant should at once gain his freedom. Peasants were to be permitted to get married without requiring their master's permission. No compensation money was to be payable to a landowner in respect of a serf girl leaving an estate on marriage.

The second proposal concerned the peasants' property rights and personal security. They should individually own the plot they cultivated, for they paid the poll tax themselves. Any property acquired by a peasant was to belong to him; no one should arbitrarily deprive him of it. The peasant was to be restored to the status of citizen. He should be judged by his equals in the lower courts, in which manorial peasants, among others, should be chosen to serve. The peasant should also be permitted to acquire real estate, that is, to buy land. Freedom was to be granted without hindrance on payment of a fixed sum to the master for a deed of manumission. Arbitrary punishment without trial was prohibited: 'Let this barbarous custom of serfdom vanish away, let the tiger's power be crushed! All this will culminate in the complete abolition of servitude.'

Radishchev's great revolutionary paragraph rings out:

'Free men who have committed no crime, in fetters, and being sold like cattle! Oh law of the land! Your wisdom exists too often in your wording alone! Is this not an open mockery of you? What is worse, this is a mockery of the sacred name of liberty. If only the slaves, weighed down by their heavy bonds, inflamed by despair, were to break our heads, the heads of their inhuman masters, with the iron which hinders their freedom, and crimson their fields with our blood! What would the country lose thereby? Soon from their midst would arise great men to replace the slain generation: but they would be inspired by a different attitude and have no right to exercise oppression. This is no fancy; my gaze pierces the thick curtain of time which hides the future from our eyes—I see through a whole century to come!'

This was no cry to raise the people to revolt. It was a warning of revolution to come. Radishchev foresaw this revolution. If the reforms he advocated had been adopted when he recommended them, it is possible that this revolution would have been averted.

Denis Fonvizin, the dramatist and satirist

The cultural criticism of society also appeared in two forms — neither necessarily linked with the abolition of serfdom. In fact two of its major exponents, Shcherbatov and Sumarokov tended to favour the institution of serfdom. In the first place, it blamed the evils in Russian society on the adoption of foreign ways and customs imported from the decadent West, typified by such general terms as 'Voltaireanism' and 'cosmopolitanism'. In the second, this criticism became, in a sense, a search for a real Russian national culture, arising from a sense of national consciousness. There took place not so much a rejection of European culture as an assimilation. The consciousness of other cultures elsewhere, and a realisation of the differences between them, made the Russian turn towards his native land and seek in turn for an essentially Russian soul. His research often caused him to look backwards, away from the unhappy present, to find the 'true' Russia in the simplicity of the pre-Petrine Muscovite period before the onset of Europeanisation.

The first line of criticism began in the theatre which was, because of its popularity, one of the most suitable media for the expression of ideas, and which gradually evolved from a court appurtenance to a powerful weapon of art and enlightenment. The movement started quietly enough by challenging the frivolity of the existing theatre: for example, Alexander Sumarokov, director of the Petersburg theatre, tried to lead Russian taste away from hedonistic Voltaireanism to the classical masters. Sumarokov was one of the best-known dramatists and literary critics of his day. He had had his early training in the Cadet

Corps where he had taken part in the cadets' Sunday dramatic performances at court and had also received a sound grounding in the French classics. His army service had ended abruptly when the success of one of his tragedies brought immediate fame culminating in his appointment to the directorship.

This theatrical criticism soon led to a small masterpiece by Denis Ivanovitch Fonvizin, variously translated as *The Adolescent*, or *The Minor*, which dealt with a contemporary Russian theme (unusual in itself in this theatre of escape)—the education of the aristocracy. First performed in 1782 at St Petersburg with the great Dmitrevsky in the cast, it depicted the upbringing of a provincial aristocrat and proved all too conclusively that western education did not, by any means, lead to enlightenment. Fonvizin also bitterly attacks the abuses of serfdom, the coarseness and ignorance of landowners, the corruption of the court and the mutilation of education and, generally, a regime where idlers and ignoramuses were the sovereign rulers of serf souls.

Nicholai Ivanovitch Novikov followed much the same lines of thought, although he was also instrumental in recalling his contemporaries to a sense of Russia's own national worth and past. His sponsorship of a national literature and his publication of a very valuable collection of historical source material were of great importance. N. I. Novikov, himself of noble birth, was notable mainly for his humanitarian concerns, as a freemason, a publisher and an editor whose activities brought him into collision with authority and made him a symbol of free thought in conflict with despotism. His successive journals—*The Drone*, *The Painter*, *The Tatler* and *The Purse*—were amongst the first organs of social criticism in Russia. They were dominated by social protest against the oppression of the peasantry and by a national protest.

In many ways, Novikov's social protest closely resembles that of Radishchev. One of his contributions, which appeared in his own journal, *The Painter*, even takes the form of an account of a journey—not from St Petersburg to Moscow, however, but simply *Fragment of a Journey to* .... It, too, is an outspoken account of what he saw—poverty and servitude, unploughed fields, ungathered harvests—and of what he found:

'That the proprietors themselves were responsible for this. Oh Humanity! You are unknown in these villages. Oh Authority! You tyrannize over

your fellow men. Oh blessed Virtue, love of one's neighbour! You are abused. The imbecile masters of these poor slaves exercise you towards horses and dogs rather than towards men.'

The Drone carried equally pointed comment. Here, for example, is a specimen purporting to be a noble's instructions to his bailiff on the correct method to deal with a famine-stricken village:

'1. Your journey from here to our estate and back to be at the expense of our village elder.

'2. On arrival you are to flog the village elder with the utmost severity in front of all the peasants for supervising the peasants slackly and letting the *obrok* fall into arrears, and then deprive him of his eldership; and furthermore extract from him a fine of 100 roubles.

'3. Discover most exactly how and in consideration of what bribes the elder deceived us with his false report. First of all have him flogged and then begin the investigation of the matter entrusted to you. . . .

'8. Settle the division of land between the peasant as you think fit, but tell them that there is to be no reduction in the *obrok* and that they must pay up promptly without any false excuses. Flog any defaulters pitilessly in front of all the peasants.'

Novikov took as his main targets the young men and women of the capitals who were blinded by their passion for foreign things to what might be good in the Russian way of life; the neglect of native art and artists merely because they were Russians or, worse still, Russian serfs; and finally, the renunciation of the Russian past—the exchange of the virtues and morals of earlier generations for the empty frivolity and superficiality of manners, morals and learning introduced by the French. In economic terms: they had bartered honest Russian goods for French frippery.

Novikov sums up the dilemma of Russian nationalism in the eighteenth century: the Russians were unwilling to return completely to the past; yet they were incapable of glorifying the present. He wished passionately to demonstrate that Russia had a dignity and greatness of its own, although he realised that Russia was not as yet entirely self-sufficient and could not live exclusively on her own cultural and intellectual

Podnovinsky suburb in Moscow during a popular feast

А САМА КДРУГЪ
ОИДУ КУРГАНЪ МЕ
ДУ ПОНЕСУ......

heritage. What he wanted, therefore, was a more discriminating reception of the West, not its rejection.

The historian and aristocrat, Prince Michael Shcherbatov, was an early exponent of a similar argument. To him, the most serious consequence of the addiction to foreign culture was the weakening of all moral bonds, specifically the bond between the citizen and the state. From here, it was an easy step to blame the peasants' ruin on the excessive luxury of the frenchified young fop, the *petimetr* (from *petit maître*) and to point to the undoubted gap between the Europeanised master and his Muscovite serf; or to follow the argument round in a full circle and say that the lessons learned abroad taught only disdain for fatherland and fellow citizens.

The fashionplates of Moscow and St Petersburg were easy targets for the pens of Russian satirists. Lacking a solid cultural foundation, the young gallants were little more than crude rustics dressed in the latest fashions. The *petimetr* had his female equivalent:

'she rides out with a coach and six accompanied by two outriders and four footmen, keeps two dozen maids and as many lackeys, eats luxuriously and always at odd hours, sleeps until noon, dresses like a singer of the St Petersburg operetta, knows only Russian, but mixes it with so many French and Italian words with Russian endings, that native Russians have a harder time understanding her than foreigners. Her conversation consists for the most part of praises of French fashions and free behaviour, she mocks pious women . . . and tries to prove that amorous adventures are possible in Moscow no less than in Paris or London.'

Another contemporary historian, Boltin, sums up the position:

'When we began to send our youth abroad and to entrust their education to foreigners, our morals entirely changed; together with the supposed enlightenment, there came into our hearts new prejudices, new passions, weaknesses and desires which were unknown to our ancestors. These extinguished in us our love for the fatherland, destroyed our attachment to the path of our fathers and to their ways. Thus we forgot the old, before mastering the new, and, losing our identity, did not become what

(opposite) *Yaroslav tile showing a young woman in western dress*

View from Ivanovsky Square in the Kremlin of the Archbis

e, the Saviour's Tower, and the St Nicholas Church

we wished to be. All this arose out of hastiness and impatience. We wanted to accomplish in a few years that which required centuries, and began to build the house of our enlightenment on sand, before having laid firm foundations.'

Sumarokov's revolt revealed the mechanism whereby the challenge imposed by the inroads of foreign culture almost forcibly led to the re-examination of Russian culture, and this search for the truly Russian culture pointed directly to the rediscovery of the Russian past. Its followers looked back through rose-coloured spectacles to the age of the Czar Fedor Alekseivitch as a time when Russians had not yet learned to mistake extravagance of dress for nobility of character. This was the starting-point for later assertions that the Muscovite period of Russian history was not inferior to the imperial period initiated by Peter the Great; that it was, in fact, with its simple beliefs and traditional practices, greatly superior. This thesis gained supporters from unexpected sources. Apart from the intelligentsia, other sections of the gentry resented the supervision and demands of the autocracy and longed to escape from the luxury, expense and loss of status of life at court. They had the happiest memories of the patriarchal village where they had reigned as undisputed masters.

This argument went hand in hand with a renaissance of interest in Russian history. Previously, the Russians of the Middle Ages were regarded as a warlike, rude and uncivilised people. Russian history, as we have said earlier, was rarely taught in schools. Only post-Petrine Russian history had been considered worthy of this new European nation. Now, the industry of modern historians brought to light traces of a superior culture in the work of the annalists which refuted the inveterate prejudice and established the probability that, previous to its subjugation by the Tartars, there was a period when the Russian nation deserved to be remembered as a civilised people. The knowledge and use of Cyrillic characters and the Slavonic translation of the Bible in the ninth century; the schools which the Grand Duke Vladimir founded and his inclination to the fine arts; the poetical paraphrase of the psalms, which began to be sang at about that time in the churches; the code of civil law which Yaroslav Vladimiravitch gave to the people of Novgorod in about 1019; the splendour of his court and lastly the monuments of painting—these were all cited as evidence of a considerable degree of indigenous Russian culture, which other European countries did not reach till much later. The Empress, as we have already seen, was instrumental in stimulating the nation's interest in its own past.

The rejection of foreign influences was extended further. The society of both capitals was considered to have abandoned the Russian traditions in exchange for an immoral and ill-considered imitation of foreign ways. Man, it was said, should turn away from urban corruption, insincerity and fecklessness and rediscover the true historic image of the nation, in the village with its isolation and permanence and in the figures of its simple but noble masters and serfs.

The process that began with the rediscovery of the village and its inhabitants, progressed to a tentative statement of their equality and arrived at a belief in their superiority and uniqueness. From the startling realisation that the peasants were also human beings, it gradually developed into the assertion that they were quite often more human than their thoughtless and cosmopolitan masters. In this way the image of the contemptible serf was converted into a symbol of national pride, the noble peasant. This theme appears again and again in the literature of the period. Radishchev rides away from the city women with these thoughts: 'On your cheeks there is rouge, on your sincerity—soot. Rouge or soot, it's all the same. I shall gallop away from you at full speed to my rustic beauties. . . . See how all my beauties' limbs are round, well-developed, straight and not contorted.' Karamzin's short story *Poor Liza* tells of a nobleman weary of the pleasures of civilised life who turns to the delights of nature in the form of a pretty peasant girl who comes to the city to sell lilies of the valley.

This interest in the people included their artistic products and was linked with the search for a national culture. There was a desire to return art to its national sources so that it might reflect the national character more faithfully. In the process, such aspects of the nation's life as its history, and the ordinary people together with their speech and their music, were admitted into literature, in disregard of eighteenth-century canons of literary taste, which demanded the exclusion of the people from all serious forms of literature. Literature had to break

A woman of Moscow

through the bounds of European classicism and reassert its own literary and historical traditions.

Popular art thus became fashionable amongst the upper classes. Radishchev speaks of folk-music as the 'soul of our people' and describes the blind folk-singer at Klin chanting his song, 'artless, but marked by touching sweetness'. Storytellers advertised their services in the *St Petersburg News*; a famous collection of *byliny* was prepared for the mill-owner, Demidov, in the middle of the century and numerous manuscript collections of folk-songs were made.

The search for a national literature went hand in hand with the search for a national language. A new burst of interest in the modernisation and secularisation of language occurred in the second half of the eighteenth century, encouraged by the Empress' own interest, by the importance attached to language as an index of culture and by the growing self-consciousness of the gentry as a class. There was a move to make Russian the language of instruction in the higher educational institutions to break the hold that foreigners possessed in the transmission of knowledge. In 1767 Kheraskov, then Rector of Moscow University, made Russian the language of instruction in all subjects.

This was one milestone. Another was passed in 1783 when the Russian Academy was founded and immediately began work on the first dictionary of the Russian language. The first volume appeared in 1789, the sixth and last in 1794; the whole contained 43,257 words.

Catherine undoubtedly assisted this movement. Apart from compiling 'complementary notes' for the first volume of the dictionary, she herself created the first children's textbook in Russian, *The Grandmother's ABC Book*, for her grandsons, Alexander and Constantine. Under the influence of her example and the encouragement of her patronage, able men of letters appeared—and also women of letters, for during her reign some 70 other women began to write—and there was an unprecedented increase in literary productivity. There was likewise great activity in the sphere of journalism, marked by the appearance of several periodicals. In 1793, there were ten foreign and some 20 Russian booksellers at St Petersburg. The number of books issued in Russia increased from 2,010 between 1751 and 1775, to 6,585 between 1776 and 1800.

Coupled with the rejection of westernisation was a rejection of St Petersburg, the western capital. St Petersburg, the creation of Peter the Great, was regarded as the personification of the foreign elements in Russian society, the home of an essentially foreign court ruled by ministers whose interests rarely coincided with those of the country as a whole. It had represented from its earliest days all that was resented and feared as strange, novel and threatening to established interests and ways of life.

It came to be considered as the antithesis of Moscow, which stood for the virtues and simplicity of an epoch which had disappeared with Peter. St Petersburg, on the other hand, represented the westernisation which the Russians must discard if they wished to retain their true identity. The abandonment of Moscow, the ancient and revered capital of Muscovite Russia, signified the abandonment of the true basis of national life. Catherine Wilmot emphasises the contrast:

'Moscow is the Imperial terrestrial, political Elysium of Russia . . . all the effective power has long since passed as an inheritance to those who rule the Imperial realm at Petersburg and flutter away their hours about the Court.'

Revolt

This movement resulted in a great upsurge of intellectual life at Moscow and the city became to some extent the capital of the intelligentsia. Until the last quarter of the eighteenth century, Moscow University had been a moribund institution with only some hundred students attending its dreary German and Latin lectures. Then, when the Russian-educated Kheraskov was rector, it became a centre of intellectual ferment and the spiritual home of Novikov and his circle. Novikov took over the Moscow University Press in 1779 and organised a public library connected with the University. Between 1781 and 1784, he printed more books at the University Press than had appeared in the entire previous 24 years of its existence. Within a decade, the number of readers of the official *University Gazette* increased from 600 to 4,000. In 1784, he began Russia's first two private printing presses, including the famous Typographical Company.

Moscow, of course, was excellently equipped for its new role. It had never become a genuinely European city despite Catherine's efforts. Its character of Asiatic mysticism was ideally suited to the centre of an anti-European movement, and its position in the heart of Russia made it a fitting focus for the search for the true Russian culture.

7 Reaction

Pugachev had been brought to Moscow in a cage and put to death. The Pugachev revolt heralded the beginning of the end of any pretence the Empress Catherine may have had to enlightened despotism. The very size and scope of the rebellion had proved to her that the two factors—enlightenment and despotism—were incompatible. If she wanted to maintain her status of despot over an enslaved nation any claim to enlightenment must be relinquished. Furthermore, the revolt had also demonstrated the terror of which the mass of the populace were capable, once unleashed from subjection. The Pugachev revolt forcibly convinced her that the nation she governed was unable to discern the subtle distinction between liberty and licence.

The events in France in the last ten years of her reign, which culminated in the Revolution, could only confirm this deduction. This was a period of great frustration for Catherine, marked by the increasing age difference between herself and her young lovers and the corresponding discrepancy between her own youthful ideas of enlightenment and the political actuality of the French Revolution.

As far as her personal life was concerned, the lover of the moment emphasised her reaction to the situation. This was one Platon Zubov, over 30 years younger than the Empress, an officer of the Imperial Guard, narrow-minded, impetuous, with a firm dislike of compromise or tolerance. His efforts to ensure Catherine's safety and his warnings about the dangers lurking at home must surely have influenced her own actions in the years when he ruled supreme in the favourite's chamber.

When considering her ideas of western enlightenment, there is no doubt that, as she consolidated her position and became more secure upon the throne, she seems to have felt a decreasing need for the façade of enlightenment to justify herself to the world. She is even found referring to the exponents of the cult as the 'half-baked sages of this age'. Furthermore, in her early years, diatribes against tyranny could be utilised to pillory her predecessors; now these tirades when published

Zubov, one of Catherine's favourites

in her empire could only be read as applying to the existing—that is to her—regime.

The fall of the Bastille and the Declaration of the Rights of Man appeared to the world as the logical culmination of the work of the Age of Enlightenment. To Catherine, they could only emphasise the fact that their enlightenment was death to herself and the regime she stood for. These last years of her reign were dedicated to preventing any suspicion of a germ from the Paris epidemic spreading in the Empire.

She withdrew hastily from all contact with the France of the Revolution. In 1790 all Russians in France were ordered to return home—and this came not a moment too soon. It had already been reported that young Paul Stroganov and his tutor, Gilbert Romney, were more than passively involved in the revolutionary movement. The following year, she decreed that French diplomatic representatives would no longer be received at her court. The Comte de Ségur, old friend that he was, had already departed in 1789. In 1793 she signed a decree breaking off diplomatic relations with France and ordered the exile of all French citizens in Russia who did not take an oath of loyalty to the Russian crown. They had to swear 'not to adhere to the impious and seditious principles now followed in France'. On the other hand, asylum was liberally given in Russia to many French royalist émigrés, until the court became a centre for an international counter-revolutionary crusade. Ships flying French flags were banned from Russian ports and Russian citizens were forbidden to travel in France, receive French newspapers or import French products.

At the same time, Catherine not only shrank in horror from any contagion with the French Revolution abroad; she dealt ruthlessly with anything that could savour, however mildly, of revolution at home. There was a sharp decline in official tolerance of the most innocuous criticism and a drive by the authorities against subversion and sedition. In this, she was ably assisted by her chief of police, Stepan Sheshkovsky, who was said to begin his interrogations by striking his victims on the jaw with his stick so that their teeth fell out. In 1790 the *Journey from Petersburg to Moscow*, which might have seemed at some other time or at some other place a harmless piece of social criticism, a travelogue, a philosophical work, now appeared as a revolutionary manifesto. Radishchev pleaded that his book was in the first place issued in a very limited edition (only about 650 copies were in fact printed) and was furthermore written in a literary style unlikely to be intelligible to the peasant masses. It was indeed, he said, only intended to convince the authorities of the pressing need for reform. To no avail. Catherine pronounced him a 'rebel worse than Pugachev . . . tainted with the French madness', and he was condemned on fictitious charges (such as attempts to harm the sovereign's health and mutinously attacking military installations), found guilty and sentenced by the Senate and High Criminal Court to death. The sentence was commuted to ten years' exile in Siberia, and from this he also obtained a reprieve when Alexander I came to the throne in 1796. He committed suicide in 1802.

Novikov, the bookseller and printer, met an almost equally harsh fate. For many years, he had been Catherine's friend and collaborator, but as the century progressed their ideas began increasingly to diverge. Even in 1777, she had taken umbrage when he, in company with other masons, had founded two schools in Petersburg, financing them with the proceeds from an innocuous journal. They had dared encroach on her private field of education. She refused to give official support to the schools or to subscribe to the journal. Her attention was also directed against his publishing house. At one point, she attempted to secure his conviction on a charge of religious heresy, but the Archbishop of Moscow refused to find grounds for indictment in the book involved—a history of religious dissent in Russia. In 1787 when famine attacked the central provinces of Russia, Novikov launched an appeal for assistance (which, incidentally, met with great success). Catherine accused him of 'trying to gain the sympathy of the lower classes'. In 1791, she finally succeeded in her attempts. Novikov was arrested, charged with trying to induce the Grand Duke Paul to join the masonic movement and planning to place Paul on the throne instead of his mother. His press and bookshop were raided and closed, his stock of books publicly burned and he was sentenced to imprisonment in the fortress of Schlusselburg for 15 years 'that there may be time for him to repent of his misdeeds'. He was pardoned by Paul I on his accession, but his health had been irremediably impaired by his confinement, and he emerged from the dungeons a broken man.

An obscure pamphleteer, Theodore Krechetov, was arrested in 1793. The investigators found that his work was 'full of thoughts about liberty' and 'might cause a breach of the peace'; he, too, was imprisoned in Schlusselburg, where he remained until 1801.

It was probably his untimely death in 1792 that saved Denis Fonvizin from a similar fate. La Harpe, Swiss tutor to the Empress' grandsons, was spared for slightly longer, though Catherine now referred to him as 'Monsieur le Jacobin'. But he, too, was shortly sent packing—though hastened on his way with a gift of 10,000 roubles and a decoration.

A strange contradiction appears here. The men that Catherine was harassing, imprisoning and banishing were in many cases the same men who in their writings were inciting Russians to turn away from France, discard French influences and search for the true Russian character. Catherine had always tacitly supported this cause. Now she was giving it active and drastic confirmation in her ban on all things French. And at the same time she was persecuting its main exponents. In a sense their anti-French argument had been confirmed. What after all could one expect of a giddy, thoughtless, urban populace other than this irresponsible bloodshed and murder?

The years 1792, which saw the assassination of Gustav II of Sweden at a masked ball, and 1793, which was marked by the execution of Louis XVI and Marie Antoinette, precipitated a witch-hunt of unprecedented violence in St Petersburg. So wild did anti-revolutionary zeal run that a French royalist general wearing a red hat was instantly arrested by an official of the police; members of the same body, many of whom could barely read, were ordered to destroy suspect books and in the process destroyed books adjacent to them in case they had been contaminated.

Even poetic transcriptions of the psalms were censored. The court poet, Gabriel RomanovichDerzhavin, was horrified to learn that the secret police had been instructed to interrogate him on his motives in writing a subversive poem. The poem in question was his paraphrase of the 82nd Psalm. The contested lines included:

Derzhavin, court poet

'Oh Kings! I imagined you to be powerful Gods; no-one is judge over you. But you, like me, have passions and are mortal just as I. And you will fall like the withered leaf from the tree and die just as the last of your slaves will die! Arise, Oh God, God of the Just, and hear their prayer. Come, Oh Judge, chastise the evil and be the one and only King of the earth!'

Fortunately, Derzhavin was able to convince his accusers that King David had written the psalm with no subversive intent towards the Empress Catherine!

All copies of an innocuous melodrama called *Vadim of Novgorod*, a former favourite of Catherine's, were burned because its nostalgic soliloquies in praise of the lost liberties of Novgorod smacked of revolutionary oratory. More understandably, the sale of the Encyclopaedia was stopped and all new Russian translations of Voltaire's work were confiscated. Finally, the police received instructions to close all masonic

Catherine in travel dress on her journey to the Crimea

lodges and even literary societies. The Society of Friends of Literary Science, a literary club to which Radishchev had belonged and which had published his articles in its journal *The Citizen in Conversation*, was closed shortly after his arrest.

Just as she had stamped out the Pugachev revolt by strengthening the position of the landowners against a possible repetition of the revolt, so she quelled the revolutionary movement before it had the remotest chance of coming to the surface. In neither case, did she pay the least heed to the actual causes.

To say that these methods succeeded is perhaps to exaggerate. Nonetheless, they did in Catherine's eyes fulfil their purpose. The French Revolution did not spread to Russia. In a way, her actions can almost be considered to have been justified. From France came new reports that the orators were 'stirring up the rabble to commit great outrages against the aristocratic class of the community', or that 'one section of His Majesty's subjects is exterminating the other with the most bestial tortures and assassinations. The mob is running amok throughout the provinces.' Already, the fall of the Bastille had been greeted with rejoicing in Russia. People had danced and embraced in the streets of St Petersburg. Inflammatory brochures had been smuggled in, translated and clandestinely circulated in manuscript copies. How could the Empress permit the possibility of even the smallest spark from the fire setting light to the great illiterate masses of her people? To most of them, France was not even a name. How much less would they have understood the complicated reasons leading to the deadly struggle between throne and people? Arson, looting and murder on a scale beyond even that witnessed during the Pugachev revolt would have been the result of any Russian assimilation of the 'alien poison'. There was no civic consciousness amongst the masses and the few intellectuals, who might have understood the reasons behind the movement, would have been swept away in the vast crowds all too ready to answer the clarion call to slake their lust for licence and destruction.

Whether Catherine the Great at this time herself understood the reasons for the French Revolution is equally doubtful. It would appear from her writings that she had grasped the fact that the events of 1789 and the years of terror which ensued were as much due to the harshness of the government in the preceding years as to the evil of the revolutionary leaders. But she never realised that the *Ancien Régime* had entirely lost its hold on the people and forfeited its very claim to survive. She believed that all that was needed to right the situation in France was a

Prince Adam Czartoryski

strong hand again at the helm. She had only to point to her own indubitably strong hand on the Russian helm as proof of her point.

To survey the situation more deeply, however, it becomes obvious that her repressive actions, though they may temporarily have appeared to have succeeded, were an entirely inadequate response to the contingencies of the moment. To have eliminated Pugachev without alleviating in any way the social disorders which gave rise to the revolt could merely postpone the day of reckoning. In the early years of her reign, Catherine appears to have understood this problem: 'If we do not consent to diminish cruelty and moderate a situation which is intolerable to the human race', she had written to her Minister of Justice, 'then sooner or later they will take this step themselves.' Yet, by her death, nothing had been accomplished towards liberating or even ameliorating the conditions of the millions of her subjects who lived in bondage. If anything, their numbers had increased and their position deteriorated during the years of her reign.

Two contemporary sources well sum up the conditions in Russia at the time of Catherine's death in 1796. Firstly, Prince Adam Czartoryski writes in his memoirs:

'The Empress Catherine who, when judged at a distance from her capital, possessed neither virtue nor even the decorum which befits a woman, succeeded in winning inside her country, especially within her capital, the veneration, even the love of her servants and her subjects.

During the long years of her reign, the army, the privileged classes, the administrators, had their days of prosperity and of glory. It is beyond doubt that since her accession, the Muscovite Empire had gained in prestige abroad and in good order at home to a far greater extent than during the preceding reigns of Anne and Elizabeth. Men's minds were still filled with antique fanaticism and with vile adoration for their autocrats. The prosperous reign of Catherine confirmed the Russians still further in their servile ways, although some rays of civilisation were by now penetrating to them.'

Count Alexander Vorontsov told Czar Alexander I in 1801:

'It is impossible to deny that the heart of Russia was drained by almost annual recruitment levies; to these were added taxes which Russia, in her immature condition, could not bear without being exhausted. . . . Immoderate luxury, indulgence in all forms of corruption, the avidity of self-enrichment and the ill-gotten gains amassed by the perpetrators of all these evils led people in 1796 almost to long for a rapid change. . . .'

Two movements had nonetheless become apparent during Catherine's latter years, both of which bore the promise of some slight improvement in the position of the serf. In the first place, the number of serfs owing only *obrok* payments to their masters was increasing and thus, though they were not by law free men, they were able to exercise a certain amount of choice in the professions they pursued. They could also augment their incomes by taking work outside the village or in factories as free hired labour. In the second place, the effects of the removal of the service obligation on the nobility coupled with Catherine's provincial government legislation were slowly appearing. A great number of landowners were gradually moving back to their estates and away from the capital. This meant that the management of the estates and the men tied to them were no longer left unsupervised, a somewhat better relationship between master and serf might have been expected and a more permanent bond between the noble and the land from which he drew his wealth could develop. It also meant the growth of provincial centres of activity; previously provincial towns had been few and far between and provincial society had consisted mainly of women and children, old people and the poorest and most ignorant of the nobles. The two capitals had been the sole centres of genuine cultural or social life. The first provincial journals in Russian history appeared in the late 1780s.

In those early years, Catherine had drawn up her own epitaph (which incidentally, was never actually employed):

'In 1744 she went to Russia to marry Peter III, 18 years of tedium and solitude caused her to read many books. When she came to the throne she wished to do good and strove to introduce happiness, freedom and prosperity.'

How far had her striving succeeded? As with all her efforts, Catherine's achievements can only be judged in the context of the landowning classes. Perhaps she saw no lower. Perhaps she did not allow her eyes to drop below to the great mass of her people. Whatever good intentions she may have turned in their direction in the early years of her reign, her actions only skimmed the surface of the population. Only when applied to them, do the words freedom, happiness and prosperity have any genuine meaning. The freedom of the nobles—if freedom can be understood as liberty to exercise power over their fellow men to the fullest—certainly increased. Their freedom to express their ideas, on the other hand, was strictly circumscribed in the last decade of the century in the face of the French terror. Their prosperity was undoubtedly given every encouragement, and similarly the prosperity of the country as an economic power reached an unprecedented level. It follows from this that their happiness must equally have grown.

But what of the freedom, happiness and prosperity of nine-tenths of the nation? Freedom as a word meant nothing to men who were the property of indifferent masters, who could be bought and sold like cattle, who could not move without permission and who could yet be moved like pieces on a chess board. Prosperity in their case once again depended on the portion their masters cared to give them. Happiness in such a situation becomes a meaningless quality. If Catherine had not been aware of their situation, her behaviour in ignoring it might have had some slight justification. After the Pugachev revolt had forced conditions to her attention, she could no longer plead ignorance as an

(opposite) *Catherine in old age*

excuse. Her actions, then, in dealing solely with the manifestation and leaving its cause untouched could only bring with it the promise of years of trouble in the future. Pugachev was brought to Moscow in a cage and put to death. The social trouble of which he was merely the personification remained.

FURTHER READING

CONTEMPORARY WRITINGS

The Russian Journals of Martha and Catherine Wilmot, 1803–8, London, 1934
N. M. Karamzin, *Letters of a Russian Traveller, 1789–1790* (tr. Florence Jonas), Columbia University, 1957
Peter Putnam (ed.), *Seven Britons in Imperial Russia, 1698–1812*, Princeton, 1952
Alexander Radishchev (tr. Leo Wiener), *A Journey from St Petersburg to Moscow*, Cambridge Mass., 1958
William Richardson, *Anecdotes of the Russian Empire* (1784), New Impression 1968 (in the series *Russia Through European Eyes*, ed. A. G. Cross, which will include other contemporary English accounts of the Age of Catherine)
Memoirs of Catherine the Great, ed. Dominique Maroger (tr. Moura Budberg), London, 1955

RECENT LITERATURE

M. S. Anderson, *Europe in the Eighteenth Century*, London, 1962
G. Scott Thomson, *Catherine the Great and the Expansion of Russia*, London, 1955
Zoé Oldenbourg, *Catherine the Great*, London, 1965
Katherine Anthony, *Catherine the Great*, London, 1931
G. P. Gooch, *Catherine the Great and Other Studies*, London, 1954
J. G. Blum, *Lord and Peasant in Russia from the Ninth to the Nineteenth Century*, Princeton, 1961
C. Marsden, *The Palmyra of the North*, London, 1942
David Lang, *The First Russian Radical, Alexander Radishchev*, London, 1959
H. Rogger, *National Consciousness in Eighteenth Century Russia*, Cambridge Mass., 1960

I would like to take this opportunity of expressing my indebtedness to the books mentioned above as well as to a large number of other contemporary sources.

Index

Figures in **bold type** refer to pages on which illustrations appear

Index

Index

Index